Social Media Marketing: Facebook Ads Edition

How to Leverage the Power of Facebook Ads to Skyrocket Any Business Or Brand You Have on Facebook, Instagram, LinkedIn, Twitter, and YouTube

By

Income Mastery

Table of Contents

Introduction

For any business born in the digital age, social media marketing has become imperative in the prospects of growing a popular or sustainable business from scratch. Once known as e-marketing, this type of marketing was once an inaccessible tool to those looking to build a loyal consumer base in the late 90s to early 2000s. But today, you can maintain a healthy growth in consumers simply by utilizing the online domain. Not only does social media allow a wider reach to people with similar interests and a necessity for your offering, but also allows for you to track progress and engagement on all marketing tools. This has inherently allowed online marketers to create and identify their brand's tone and image through its digital presence.

Social media marketing doesn't only allow an increased visibility to a broader audience, but allows what many consumers want from their brands inherently today - interaction. If a consumer feels like they can personally interact with a company on social media, they feel more inclined to contributing to their success. Often times, consumers will even share these interactions to their social circles, which creates further business thanks to the word of mouth. And if a brand can convey personality in those interactions, then customers tend to share even more and relay said interactions. This passive kind of marketing is what builds sustainable businesses and brands today.

If we were to take a look at a competitive market like the fast food industry, you can distinctly distinguish the tone in their respective personalities from their Twitter and Facebook accounts. While some may present a cheeky image on their social media accounts to cater to younger and more active digital users, others could approach their interactions more conventionally without much humor. But this is the beauty and power of social media marketing. Online your brand can be anything it wants to be and attract a distinct audience based off of your approach to how you market digitally.

Digital advertising isn't anything new as television and news advertisers often targeted a specific audience. For instance, advertisers of a new cooking item would often targeted cooking programs or culinary publications. This isn't anything new. The only difference is that this new age of social media marketing is more precise in its targets and can often find niche markets for your business. But with audiences becoming wiser to the approach of traditional advertisers, social media allows you to approach consumers more authentically since they're already on a platform occupied by the people they know and love. Especially with ads targeting their interests directly, they are more likely to click on these ads than the incidental ones provided on non-targeted platforms. This is imperative for new and small business' who desire that organic "word-of-mouth" quicker and more efficient with targeted interested groups known as hyper-targeting.

Facebook Advertising has been the leading player in hyper-targeting ads since its inception in 2007. The specialty about Facebook's approach to this kind of marketing is that - even with over 2.2 billion people being on the platform - it's micro-targeting will find the exact audience for your business or brand. While Twitter and other social media platforms have advertising services, Facebook is a major part of many people's social lives. It is also the only marketer in the digital space that directly seeks users who are looking for the same interests to your business. And with over 1.5 billion daily active users and 78% of American consumers saying they discovered their products on Facebook, it's no wonder why digital ads on Facebook account for 51% of the total advertising spent in the United States.

Facebook advertising is the new frontier and in this guide, we will teach you how to leverage the platform to secure the online audience you need to skyrocket your brand to new heights.

Chapter 1: What is Facebook Advertising?

With over 2.3 billion people using Facebook daily, Facebook Advertisements is a hyper-targeting advertising service provided by Facebook. Created in 2007, ads are typically shown to Facebook users based on consumer activity including pages they've liked, places they've checked while using the platform, and information on their profile. So while similar to digital-based advertising programs like Google AdSense, Facebook Ads is tailored made to its users and their particular interests. Their system also places higher priority on what the advertisers desired audience is and then match those to their said interests. For example, if a bike company is desiring to target bike enthusiasts, Facebook will target users the have that have interests in cycling listed on their profile. Facebook Ads can also target age, location, gender, and mobile users, which other platforms are unable to do. This is why Facebook Ads are the number one marketer with over 84% of all engagement and clicks on Internet ads being linked back to Facebook's advertisement platform.

Often before advertisers create a Facebook Ad, it's wise to understand what exactly the program is and how it works. Unlike other platforms, Facebook Ads are auction-based meaning that advertisers are charged on impressions and clicks rather than paying upfront. There are also many types of ads to choose from with the central two category being ads and sponsored stories. Businesses will often create and publish their ads either through Facebook's Ad creation portal or utilize their own API developer. The simplicity of Facebook's self-service ad creating interface is also a draw to the platform for new businesses since it's step-by-step process is easy to use.

Types of Ads

As mentioned previously, Facebook has two Ad categories: Ads and Sponsored. In the Ads category, there are 6 different advertisement types that exist. Although it can seem quite overwhelming at first, each ad has a significant purpose and are all based on their placement on the website.:

1. Domain Ads

2. Desktop App Ads

3. Carousel Ads

4. Dynamic Product Ads

5. Instant Experience Ads

6. Collection Ads

7. Messenger Ads

8. Engagement Ads (Page Like Ads, Page Post Photo Ads, Page Post Text Ads)

9. Offer Claim Ads

10. Facebook Lead Ads

Domain Ad

Domain ads are advertisements that you would find on the side of your Facebook screen. It is called Domain ads because it quite literally takes you to an online domain once you click on them. Domain ads are also the most likely to receive a impression on the platform since it is classically known and quickly tells consumers what is being advertised. A simple click will take you to the website and be considered an impression for the advertiser.

Desktop App Ads

Desktop App Ads are ads used to drive consumers to your built-in apps in Facebook. Facebook apps tend to be targeted towards older audiences who are more likely to use the platform on desktops, since it is still available on mobile.

Carousel Ads

Carousel Ads (also known as multi-product ads) is a slideshow format of ads that allows advertisers to show 10 moving or stationary images and lines in a single ad template. This type of ad is typically for those trying to promote multiple products from a store or use multiple posts as a trial to see what works best with their desired audience.

Dynamic Product Ads

Dynamic Product Ads allows you to target and track consumers previous actions on your website and inundate Facebook users with precisely timed ads based on their interests. Facebook does an exquisite job on detailing this type of ad:

"Dynamic ads look similar to other ads on Facebook, Instagram, and Messenger. However, instead of individually creating an ad for each of your products, you create an ad template that automatically uses images and details from your data feed for things you'd like to advertise. Dynamic ads utilize your Facebook Pixel to show ads to people who have already shown interest in your business by taking actions you care about on your site."

The attraction to this type of ad by many advertisers is its unique personalization and attack on those special groups of merchants. It's also the most effective ad-type on the platform and provides the best rate of return due to its targeting strategy. It also requires the least upkeep because once the initial ad is set-up by the advertiser, the algorithm does the rest. These ads can only be used buy merchants who upload their entire product inventory on Facebook and then install Facebook Pixel on your site's pages (see more information in the Facebook Pixel chapter).

Instant Experience Ads

Instant Experience Ads (also known Canvas Ads) are mobile-only supported interactive ads that allow users to do everything swiping through a slideshow to zooming , tilting , and moving into scenes or images with the touch of their fingers. Instant Experience Ads has often been marketed as being able to load 10 times fast than mobile web applications since it can be linked to Facebook Pixels

Collection Ads

Collection ads can also only be used on mobile devices. These ads allow users to buy products without leaving the confines of Facebook. It is often grouped with Instant Experience Ads, so that users are able to go directly to the marketer's store to make purchases.

Messenger Ads

Messenger ads are quite simply ads that are directly built into the Facebook Messenger app and desktop portal.

Engagement Ads - Page Post Link, Photo, and Text Ads

Engagement ads are sponsored posts that are either featured on the feed of Facebook users or on the right hand side of the feed. These are also known as any of the original or classic ads that was featured on Facebook since the website began.

Offer Claim Ads

Offer Claim Ads are most often used to promote a discount or special deal on one of your products. These ads can also be targeted towards those who have clicked into your ad or website, but have not committed to any purchases. They can traditionally appear as an image, carousel, or video.

Facebook Lead Ads

Lastly, Facebook Lead Ads are the website's most dynamic and useful for marketers considering the amount of market research and consumer feedback that the tool provides advertisers. While majorly optimized for mobile devices, lead ads present users with a form that is typically pre-populated with details from their Facebook profile. The remainder of the form can be completed in several quick tapes. As previously mentioned, the form is optimized for mobile since 88% percent of Facebook's user are on digital handheld devices and the taking 40 percent longer to complete on desktop computers.

Facebook Lead Ads are also highly attractive for users because they often feature compelling features that are not featured on the others ads on the website. From providing users incentives from deals and sweepstakes to product samples and ability to join a mailing list, the Lead Ads are the most direct in its interactive nature since consumers are able to answer questions themselves. While other hyper-targeting ads on the website may passively analyze consumer habits and interests, this tool directly ask users of their interests in particular products and more.

Facebook Lead Ads can be more involved for advertisers like yourself than other ad-types, which why we've listed the 10 steps for setting up Facebook Lead Ads.

Creating Facebook Lead Ads

1. Go to the Ads Manager.
2. Once you are in the Ads Manager, select Create in the lop left corner and click Lead

generation. Here you will be able to name your campaign.

3. Choose the Facebook Page that you would like to utilize as your Lead Ad. Select View Terms and agree on the Terms & Conditions once you've reviewed them.

4. Here you will select your target audience, budget, schedule, and placements. It is also worth noting that Lead Ads cannot be targeted to people under the age of 18.

5. Choose your Lead Ad format, which can be an image, video, slideshow, or carousel.

6. Preview your Lead Ad on the right-hand side. Add your headline, body copy, and call to action.

7. Scroll to the bottom of your screen and click Contract Form. Here you will be able to add an intro, custom questions, form title, your company's privacy policy, and thank you screen.

8. Once you've filled in the details of the form to your liking, select Settings under the name of your form to make sure that you collect organic leads. While optional, this is highly recommended.

9. Select Finish and review your ad from Facebook Ads Manager. Once ready to publish, click Confirm.

10. Congratulations! You have successfully created a Facebook Lead Ad and now either implement them through Facebook's Marketing API or do a manual download. Remember to always keep your form simple and to add incentives for users to want to partake in the form for a higher rate of interaction.

Now with the knowledge in understanding Facebook Advertising, you are ready to get started.

Chapter 2: How to Get Started with Facebook Advertising?

With organic "word-of-mouth" seemingly going by the wayside with savvier consumers, an efficiently ran Facebook Ads campaign is a necessity in today's age. So let's get started by taking you through the steps on how to get an effective Facebook Ads campaign started on the platform.

It's imperative that you start a Facebook Business Page in order to begin capitalizing off of your first Facebook ad campaign. Facebook Business Page are the new home for all eCommerce and 'brick-and-mortar' businesses as they provide a home for online clients to explore your business from the comfortability of a platform they are already familiar with. Once you've created a business, you can now go to the Facebook Ads Manager to create your first ad campaign.

Next, it's important to choose a marketing objective, so that you can clearly know in what direction you want to take you brand awareness. This can be done by selecting the Campaigns tab, and then Create to start your new ad. Now Facebook offers over 11 objectives for you to choose from based on what you want your ads to accomplish:

- Brand awareness: Introduces your brand to a new audience.
- Reach: Reaches as many users as possible on Facebook.
- Traffic: Drives traffic to a specific web address or mobile app.
- Engagement: Focuses on audience reach to increase the number of post or likes, encourage people to claim an offer, or increase attendance at your event, or encourage.
- App installs: Influences users to install your app.
- Video views: Influences users to view your videos.
- Lead generation: Inspires new consumers into your sales funnel.
- Messages: Inspires users to contact your business through Facebook Messenger.
- Conversions: Influences people to take action on your website.
- Catalog sales: Connects your Facebook ads to your product catalog to show users ads they will most likely buy.
- Store visits: Sends nearby customers to bricks-and-mortar stores.

Once you choose your desired ad objectives, you're all ready to move on to naming your campaign. Scroll to the bottom of your Facebook ad campaign where you will be able to choose a name and select if you would like for budget optimization to be selected. This is quite useful if you are using multiple sets of Facebook ads, but if you are not - then you can leave it off. If you selected the Engagement objective, there is one more step - where you will be able to choose between post engagement, page likes, and event responses. Once this is selected, click on Set Up Ad Account and move on to the next step.

Now you will be able to set up your contrary, time zone, and preferred currency. These details are imperative to the type of audience you are trying to target. These account details can also not be changed. You will have to create an entirely new ad account in order to do so. So choose your key account details wisely during this step.

After you've successfully set up your account, you're ready to target your audience by scrolling down to the building your Custom Audience. Select your target age, gender, location, and location and then look at the audience size indicator - which will tell you your potential reach. This is important in analyzing your previous set objectives. If your potential ad reach is smaller than originally intended, it may be wise to change your target demographics accordingly. This will help you gain more of a potential ad reach.

Time and time again, we've mentioned that Facebook Ads are known for their hyper-targeting strategy. Here is where you finally choose in which way you would like to hyper-target those audiences. Detailed targeting allows you to specifically include or even exclude users based on their behaviors, interests, and demographics. Connections allows you include or exclude users who have a connect your Facebook Page, app or event you've previously managed. These hyper-targeting features enables you to really attack any specific market that you desire.

Once you've chosen a way to target your audience, now you are able to move onto your ad placement. Now if you are new to Facebook advertisements, you can certainly do automatic placements and Facebook will trot your ads to all its services until it finds the best results. But if you know exactly where you would like to place your Facebook ads, you do have options ranging from different device types (mobile, desktop, or both) to platforms including iOS, Android, or Facebook's many interfaces including Instagram. We will discuss more about Instagram in later chapters, but the ability to be able to target different audiences is up.

Next, you will be able to set your schedule and budget. You will also be able to decide what you want to spend on your ads by setting a daily or lifetime budget. There are also advanced options in defining how much you would like to spend, but this is all based on your personal preferences. Setting a schedule rather than running your ads all the time can present ads to your specified target audience more directly. Once you are happy with your decision, you are finally ready to move on to the final step.

Lastly, you are ready to create your ad and choose an ad format. You can scroll through all the available formats that are provided to see which format looks best for your product or advertisement. It's also important to use the preview tool here to see how your ad will look on different devices and platforms. It's also to note the different specs listed under each platform, so that your ad doesn't look unprofessional. But once you are all set, you can click Confirm and wait until Facebook has approved your ad.

Congratulations! While the Facebook Ad Approval process can take anywhere from five minutes to two days, you have just completed the hardest part in creating your Facebook Ad.

Chapter 3: What is Facebook Ads Manager?

With over 1.4 billion people using Facebook daily and 91% of advertisers investing in Facebook Ads in the past year, it can be quite overwhelming in the thought of connecting to an audience. But the great thing about Facebook is that no matter who your audience is, you can reach them through Facebook Ads network. This is where Facebook Ads Manager comes into play. Sure it can be quite intimidating when first using the service. But it's an amazing tool that will help you deliver successful campaigns to your audience. Now that we have an understanding of the intention of the platform, let's get started in setting Facebook Ads Manager up.

To begin, go to the drop-down menu on the corner of any Facebook page and select Manage Ads. You can also directly access this page from the Facebook Ads Manager app. Once in, you will be brought to an Ads account page where you will see an rundown of your ad account. If you have multiple ad accounts, you will be able to see each of your campaigns listed as well as the Status of you ad, Spend Cap, Spend Cap Remaining, and Spent amount already. You can also add teammates to help manage and create ads via the ads account without giving them direct access to your personal or business page.

If you're ready to build your team, go into your settings, click on the menu in the top-left hand corner and then select Ad Account Settings. Choose Account Roles and select Add a User to add a new member to your team and account. You can also assign appropriate roles including Admin, Advertiser, and Analyst. Each role only has certain permissions and capabilities.

An Ad account Analyst can only see ad performance and is typically of anyone on your team who is creating reports on your Facebook Ads. The can only see ads. An Ad account Advertiser can do all the things an Analyst can do, but they can also use payment methods for your ads. They can also create and edit ads in this capacity. This is something an Analyst is not able to do. Ad account Advertisers are typically for anyone doing freelance for your project or a partner agency helping with development.

The last role is Ad account Admin , which is the ultimate role on the platform. On top of doing everything analyst and advertisers can do, they can also manage roles, access permission in the account and control overall ad spending (including adding limits). It's also worth noting that roles on a Facebook Page, Facebook Business Manager, and ad account are not the same. You can have full access to edit a Facebook Page, but not have access to do anything on a company's ad account. This is why its important to hand these roles out to the proper team members

Now that we have spoken on the roles for your Ad account. we will discuss how to create and edit ads.

Creating Ads

To start creating your ads, select the green Create Ad button in the top right corner of your Facebook Ads Manager. After you select the create a new ad button, you'll have over 15 different objective, such as promoting your Facebook page, boosting posts, and installing your app. The creation of your ads is pretty explanatory on the site, but we explain how in later chapters how to create the perfect ads.

Editing Ads

Once you begin creating ads, there are going to be times that you want to increase the budget of your ad or change the wording of the text. Instead of starting a new campaign, you can edit existing Facebook ads by having over the ad name and click the Edit icon. A pop-up will then come up that will give you the option to edit a single ad, ad set, or campaign. A unique feature that Facebook Ads has adde recently is the ability to edit multiple campaigns and ads at once. To do this, just check the boxes in the first column and select Edit on the navigation bar that will appear above.

For ads, you can edit the ad name, edit the destination for the ad, edit the image, text, or link of the ad, and turn the ad on or off if you want it to go inactive. For ad sets, you will be able to edit the target audience, ad placement, ad set name, the budget and schedule, and the optimization and intended audience for the ad. For campaign, you'll be able to edit the campaign name, set spending limits, or make the entire campaign active or inactive. These decisions will be provided once you select Edit on the navigation bar for the respective

Ad Reports

Now traditionally, Facebook advertisers will have a social media goal in order to see how their ads are performing against their set goals. So if the purpose of your Facebook ad is to encourage signups for your product, you can see which one of your campaign is driving the most signups, how many people signed up through your ads, and what those signups are costing you. Facebook ads allows you to do this. Its reports through Facebook Ads Manager will allow you to filter results and create a report for your team to analyze what is working or not working.

Ad Report Filters

Facebook gives you four easy ways to filter through your ads. Search, Filters, Date Range, and Ad Tier will allow you to decipher what exactly you want to see and analyze to create better ads.

Search

This is quite explanatory as you will be able to search your ads by anything from Campaign Name to Ad Name.

Filters

You can filter your ads more exclusively by the following:

- Saved Filters – Filters you have created and saved previously

- Delivery – The status of your ads
- Objective – What your ad is optimized for (i.e. Brand awareness or conversions)
- Buying Type – How you pay for your ads (i.e. Auction or fixed price)
- Placement – Where your ads appear (i.e. Facebook right column or Instagram)
- Metrics – Specific measures for your ads (i.e. Lifetime spent less than $50)
- Date Updated – When your ads were last updated.

Date Range

Date range can be adjusted to today, yesterday, last 7 days, last 14 days, last 30 days, last month, this month and lifetime. You can also customary set your date range in order to see what has worked best with your ads.

Ad Tier

Advertisers can choose to filter by ad tier as well by going to the dashboard on the left hand side and toggling between all campaigns, all ad sets, and all ads. This will allow you to apply multiple filers at once. For instance, you can search for all your ads sets with the objective of

'Conversions' and lifetime spend of less than $50 in the past 30 days.

You can also choose to save these custom filters for the future. The button to do so is to the right of the gray filter bar marked Save Filter. This will give you quick access in the future.

Stats, Filters, and More Data

Facebook Ads can provide its users an overwhelming amount of data and allow you to customize you own report tables. There are two central ways that you can customize your reporting table through Columns and Breakdowns. To help you find relevant data, there are several presets of columns that you will be able to choose from:

- Performance: Results, Reach, Costs, Amount Spent, etc.
- Delivery: Reach, Frequency, CPM, Impressions, etc.
- Engagement: People Taking Action, Reactions, Comments, Shares, etc.
- Video Engagement: Impressions, 3s Video Views, etc.

- App Engagement: Mobile App Installs, Mobile App Actions, Cost per Mobile App Install, etc.
- Carousel Engagement: Reach, Frequency, Impressions, Clicks, etc.
- Performance and Clicks: Results, Reach, Cost, etc.
- Cross-Device: Website Actions, Mobile Apps Install, Website Action, Conversion Value, etc.
- Messenger Engagement: Link Clicks, Messaging Replies, Blocked Messaging Conversations, etc.
- Offline Conversions: Purchase, Purchase Conversion Value, Cost per Purchase, etc.

If none of the presents that Facebook Ads has created suits your needs, you can certainly create your own. Do this by selecting Customize Columns… in the 'Columns: Performance' drop down menu. A pop-up will then appear on your screen where you will be able to choose which performance metrics you would like to be analyzed. The data you choose can then be sorted by clicking on the heading of each column.

Understanding Ad Performance

A common theme in understanding ad performance is seeing exactly how effective your ads are to the audience that you are trying to captivate. Luckily, Facebook Ads Manager allows you to customize your data to provide your the most detailed information to obtain the best results from your ads. To do so, select the name of your ad on the Facebook Ads Manager. You will be able to see an Insights Graph, Summary, and Reporting Table.

The **insights graph** gives you a visualization of your ads data and an overview on how your ad is doing. There are three tabs featured here as well: Performance, Demographics, and Placement.

Performance will tell you the performance of your advertisement over a selected date range. There are several preset graphs showing you the results of your ads including its objective, reach, and amount spent on the ad. As mentioned before, you can customize the graphs to compare two things at once.

Demographics will allow you to see the gender and age breakdown of the data in your ad. You can click into the tab to see results on impressions, reach, and amount spent. Impressions is different from the reach under the demographics tab. Impressions is how many times the ad is seen, while reach is how many people saw the ad.

Placement shows how your ad has performed across Facebook's many platforms including Instagram and placements on the site like on the left column of the desktop or on a mobile feed. You can view how many likes an ad got, impressions, reach, and amount spent across its many platforms.

The **summary section** will give you summaries on your ad including delivery, amount spent today, total schedule, and overall objective. This is also where you will be able to make you ad inactive, edit your ad, or create a similar ads. You can delete your ad in this section as well.

The **reporting table** is a dashboard that displays information about your ad, ad set, or campaigns. It will not allow you to see all your Facebook ads though. So, if you are viewing a campaign, you will only be able to see the ads and ad sets in a campaign. Similarly, if you are viewing an ad, you will only be able to see that ad.

Other Features on Facebook Ads Manager

Lastly, Facebook Ads Manager has many other features that could be helpful in identifying your audience for your ads.

Audience Insights

The Audience Insight tool will give you more of an understanding for your audience in a clear and accessible way. It collects information regarding the audience's demographics, location, behaviors, and more. You can even click the green Create Ad button to create an ad that targets this specific audience.

Pixels

We'll discuss Facebook Pixels in later chapters, but the platform will allow you to track and analyze the success rate of who has visited your site based on your Facebook Ads. To create this and begin tracking conversions, go to your Facebook Ads menu and click Pixels under Assets.

Power Editor

Typically, not for beginners of Facebook Ads, Power Editor is for marketers who want to create larger amounts of ads at once while maintaining specific control over how the ads are served. Power Editor can be accessed by going to the Facebook Ads menu and looking under Create & Manage.

Facebook Ads Manager Mobile Apps

Don't forget that you can also manage all these features and tools on any iOS and Android mobile device. Albeit limited features, you can manage campaigns, create ads, check metrics, and even get notifications for your ad's performance. This final feature could be vital if you are focused on hyper-analyzing and tracking how well you ad is doing.

Simply put, when used properly Facebook Ads Manager can be a key component to the success of any ad. From customizable features to highly detailed reports, your ads can thrive on Facebook if you analyze the performance closely enough in cultivating the very best adverts for your desired audience.

Chapter 4: Boosting a Facebook Post and Its Perks

With Facebook users traditionally using the platform on a daily basis, you may see decline in the organic reach of your posts. This is typical for any business. Although you can promote a new ad on Facebook, it can only go so far organically as you are competing with a myriad of other advertisers and marketers on the playoutform.

This is where Facebook boost comes in handy.

The feature is available to anyone who has access to Facebook Business Page, but the feature is quite simply paying more to get your content seen by more people. And the great thing is that it won't hurt your ad metrics since it is just being redistributed to a similar target audience who has engaged in your app previously. It's also easy to use. The tool allows your to select Boost Post and your content will go live almost instantaneously. Sure, Facebook has to re-review the post before they release it to your audience. But once they do, you'll begin reaching new people. Also, don't forget that boosted posts can be anything from images, videos, messages, and links to website. It's a new way that you'll be able to engage with an audience that you didn't know existed. There are also some other perks to boosted posts as well.

The biggest perk is what the purpose of boosted posts has always been which is to reach a much wider audience beyond those who are already subscribed to you. As mentioned before, you can also set the criteria for the types of users you would like to interact with your post. You can also narrow your boosted post to target a very specific demographic that may be different than your other posts. Boosted posts seemingly allow you to test a new audience in a hyper-quick way than usual.

Facebook boosted posts will also give you control once your post does go live, which is a great addition. So if you want to end the planned boost run short after seeing unimpressive analytical returns, and boost another post instead - you can do that. And with Facebook Insights, you will be given a very detailed summary of how your boosted posts are doing. In order to see this, go to the Insights tab, and select Posts. Once here, you'll be able to see a breakdown of your post in terms of clicks and interactions. You will also be able to boost other posts from this page if you see that your boosted post is doing so well.

It's wise to remember that you can boost almost anything that is featured on your Business

Page. From announcements to call-of-actions, you're able to promote something that may have underperformed to your desired audiences. Besides the audience, Facebook Boost gives three features:

- Audience - You are able to set criteria for the individuals who see your boosted posts, including demographics like age, location, and interests. And alluded to before, you can create custom audiences or lookalike audiences on people who've already responded positively to your ad before.
- Budget - You're able to control exactly how much you spend on this boost, but your budget can always
- Duration - All ads can be run at a fixed period or be manually turned off. So if you're happy with its performance after only a day's run, you're more than welcome to stop the boosted post.

Now like any form of marketing, boost posts do cost money. But instead of paying for placement and paying up front, you'll be setting up your ads via a budget. You will be able to tell the platform exactly how much you want. The minimum budget is $1 per day, but remember the more you pay, the more audience members you are going to get to see your post. It's also worth mentioning that these paid boosts do not mean guaranteed engagement. It solely means that more eyes will see your product or service. So it's very important that you understand this before committing a lot of money to boosting your ad. Luckily, Facebook will give you an estimated number of how many people will see you ad for each budget level and plugged in target audience. This means that the reach numbers will vary based upon who you're targeting. So while a similar brand post may have received a better reach, it may be wise to relook at your target audience. This will help you get a better reach.

How to Boost a Facebook Post

Step One

Select a Facebook Post to boost. If you are creating a post and then boosting it, select the grey Boost Post button on the bottom right corner of the post box. If you are boosting an existing post, select the blue Boost Post in the bottom right. You can also go to the Insights tab and preview a list of posts that will each have a Boost Post feature next to it.

Step Two

Target an audience. You can opt to only include people currently by default or all current followers and their friends. But you will find that it is better to target specific demographics based on location, gender, and interests. You can create a custom audience for your boosted post by click Create New Audience. This will give you the ability to target and define audiences how you want to.

Step Three

Set your budget. Since your audience is set, you'll have the ability to properly analyze the reach of your post under a certain budget tier. While you can stretch your budget across however many days you want, just remember that the minimum budget is $1 per day.

Step Four

Set the length of your boost. By default, Facebook will allow you to choose between running your boost between one, seven, or fourteen days. But you can also choose to run your ads through a specified date in the future. This is all based on your budget and expectations for your reach.

Step Five

Review your post. This may be the most important step of the process because it allows you to check your ad copy for errors. You can also ensure that your links properly work and your visuals are showing up properly. The worst thing that can happen when apply these boosts is having a part of your ad cut off due to resizing or utilization of a different platform. Remember that your ad has to not only be functional on desktop, but mobile devices as well. So make sure it's functional before going live.

Step Six

Choose a payment option. Now you are ready to pay for your boost.Facebook accepts all payment types as you might expect, so fill in all your details and you're ready to go.

Step Seven

Boost your posts. Now you are ready to get your boosted post reviewed by Facebook and get published. It's important here to check back from time to time to check the status of your post. If your ad has not been accepted, Facebook will often give back notes on why this is the case.

More Tips & Tricks for Boosted Posts

- Remember to not get too rigid in your preferred demographics and strategies. Experiment with other choices and understand that this is your time to do this since you're not only hyper-targeting users - but doing show in higher rates than ever. This will help your refine your ads going forward even if these boosted posts don't get you the audience conversions you expected. You were still able to learn from your previous mistakes and build better ads in the future.

- It's also important to narrow your audiences as much as possible. With narrower criteria and more specific posts, you'll be able to connect more with audiences and create relevance between the posts and their intended targets.

- While Facebook does allow you to run boosted ads for as long as you want, it's important to not run the same ad for too long. An ad will likely see a decline in results after a week of running. So you can manually turn off your ads, reset, and begin another boosted post.

- During this time, experiment with different ads that you wouldn't traditionally try. By having a different ad being boosted, you may find great results in finding a different audience and new set durations. You can also study how these new ads did to previous ads since Facebook Ads will give you access to all your historical data.
- This may seem like a no brainer, but automatically boosting your highest performing posts to save time can make a huge difference in engagement. Because this ad has already connected with an audience, an extended reach will only make your proven ad more successful and your contributed budget more resourceful.

With these steps and tricks, you will be able to reach thousands of new audiences with your boosted ad posts. And you can often do so with only a few dollars. It's one of the most important tools to utilize when attempting to get the most out of your Facebook campaign and earning more traffic to your website.

Chapter 5: Facebook Ad Guidelines and Policies

So why aren't your Facebook Ads getting approved?

This is a common question for new Facebook Ad users. After putting hours and hours of work into market research, choosing the best ad format, and learning the advertising program, you get rejected for posting your first advertisement. Fortunately, Facebook's Ad Guidelines and Policies are listed on the website to help you revise your Ad to m. And we've chosen the most common reasons why an Ad is not successful in being approved on the platform.

Often, problems in your ad can be creatively including having too much text featured in your image. Bizarrely, this is the number one reason why ads are rejected on the service. It used to be that if text covered more than 20% of the ad space then it was instantly denied, but now it's based on how much of the image you have featured in the Ads. There's also a new age text acceptability toggle that will tell you if you imagine is 'OK' to "High" risk of being denied based on how much text is featured.

Furthermore, while hyper-targeting is the name of the game with all Facebook ads - you are unable to target personal attributes in Facebook users. This means that it may be wise to restrain from even using words like "you" and "yours" in your advertisement. Facebook has also issued that personal attributes includes race, ethnic origin, religion, beliefs, age, sexual orientation or practices, gender identity, disability, medical condition (including physical or mental health), financial status, membership in a trade union, criminal record, or even someone's name. Although Facebook encourages hyper-targeting, they want businesses to target those through their algorithms rather than the wording in your ads.

You also cannot target others by using or manipulating Facebook's logo to garner attention and misuse your association in the brand. It's best to stay away from any tactics of manipulation when creating your advert and being organic in simply showing your product to potential users. This means that your ad also has to promote and be exactly what it is. Facebook will instantly deny any ads that features a URL that doesn't match the URL of the landing page. This means that you can't promote "www.puppyvideos.com" and take users to a site about tobacco products. It's also wise to check your URL before submission because Facebook will even deny an ad if there's a typo in the link to the website.

Lastly if your Facebook Ad still isn't being approved, it's simply because it doesn't match up with the platform's community standards. From bad grammar to short-term loan services, you would be surprised of the types of ads that are unable to be featured on the website and those have been listed below.

Illegal Products or Services

Ads must not constitute, facilitate, or promote illegal products, services or activities. Ads targeted to minors must not promote products, services, or content that are inappropriate, illegal, or unsafe, or that exploit, mislead, or exert undue pressure on the age groups targeted.

Discriminatory Practices

Ads must not discriminate or encourage discrimination against people based on personal attributes such as race, ethnicity, color, national origin, religion, age, sex, sexual orientation, gender identity, family status, disability, medical or genetic condition.

Tobacco Products

Ads must not promote the sale or use of tobacco products and related paraphernalia.

Drugs & Drug-Related Products

Ads must not promote the sale or use of illegal, prescription, or recreational drugs.

Unsafe Supplements

Ads must not promote the sale or use of unsafe supplements, as determined by Facebook in its sole discretion.

Weapons, Ammunition, or Explosives

Ads must not promote the sale or use of weapons, ammunition, or explosives. This includes ads for weapon modification accessories.

Adult Products or Services

Ads must not promote the sale or use of adult products or services, except for ads for family planning and contraception. Ads for contraceptives must focus on the contraceptive features of the product, and not on sexual pleasure or sexual enhancement, and must be targeted to people 18 years or older.

Adult Content

Ads must not contain adult content. This includes nudity, depictions of people in explicit or suggestive positions, or activities that are overly suggestive or sexually provocative. Ads must also not assert or imply the ability to meet someone, connect with them or view content created by them must not be positioned in a sexual way or with an intent to sexualize the person featured in the ad.

Third-Party Infringement

Ads must not contain content that infringes upon or violates the rights of any third party, including copyright, trademark, privacy, publicity, or other personal or proprietary rights.

Sensational Content

Ads must not contain shocking, sensational, disrespectful or excessively violent content.

Personal Attributes

Ads must not contain content that asserts or implies personal attributes. This includes direct or indirect assertions or implications about a person's race, ethnic origin, religion, beliefs, age, sexual orientation or practices, gender identity, disability, medical condition (including physical or mental health), financial status, membership in a trade union, criminal record, or name.

Misleading or False Content

Ads, landing pages, and business practices must not contain deceptive, false, or misleading content, including deceptive claims, offers, or methods.

Controversial Content

Ads must not contain content that exploits controversial political or social issues for commercial purposes.

Non-Functional Landing Page

Ads must not direct people to non-functional landing pages. This includes landing page content that interferes with a person's ability to navigate away from the page.

Surveillance Equipment

Ads may not promote the sale of spy cams, mobile phone trackers or other hidden surveillance equipment.

Grammar & Profanity

Ads must not contain profanity or bad grammar and punctuation. Symbols, numbers and letters must be used properly without the intention of circumventing our ad review process or other enforcement systems.

Nonexistent Functionality

Ads must not contain images that portray nonexistent functionality. This includes imagery that replicates play buttons, notifications, or checkboxes, as well as ads containing features that do not work, such as multiple choice options in the ad creative itself.

Personal Health

Ads must not contain "before-and-after" images or images that contain unexpected or unlikely results. Ad content must not imply or attempt to generate negative self-perception in order to promote diet, weight loss, or other health related products.

Payday Loans, Paycheck Advances, and Bail Bonds

Ads may not promote payday loans, paycheck advances, bail bonds, or any short-term loans intended to cover someone's expenses until their next payday. Short term loan refers to a loan of 90 days or less.

Multilevel Marketing

Ads promoting income opportunities must fully describe the associated product or business model, and must not promote business models offering quick compensation for little investment, including multilevel marketing opportunities.

Penny Auctions

Ads may not promote penny auctions, bidding fee auctions, or other similar business models.

Counterfeit Documents

Ads may not promote fake documents, such as counterfeit degrees, passports or immigration papers.

Low Quality or Disruptive Content

Ads must not contain content leading to external landing pages that provide an unexpected or disruptive experience. This includes misleading ad positioning, such as overly sensationalized headlines or prompts for users to inauthentically interact with the ad, and leading people to landing pages that contain minimal original content and a majority of unrelated or low quality ad content.

Spyware or Malware

Ads must not contain spyware, malware, or any software that results in an unexpected or deceptive experience. This includes links to sites containing these products.

Automatic Animation

Ads must not contain audio or flash animation that plays automatically without a person's interaction or expands within Facebook after someone clicks on the ad.

Unauthorized Streaming Devices

Ads must not promote products or items that facilitate or encourage unauthorized access to digital media.

Circumventing Systems

Ads must not use tactics intended to circumvent our ad review process or other enforcement systems. This includes techniques that attempt to disguise the ad's content or destination page.

Prohibited Financial Products and Services

Ads must not promote financial products and services that are frequently associated with misleading or deceptive promotional practices.

Sale of Body Parts

Ads must not promote the sale of human body parts or fluids.

Chapter 6: How to Setup Facebook Pixel

So now you've set up your Facebook Ads account, it'll be wise to fill you in on another service that Facebook provides to help assist with tracking your ad audience. Facebook Tracking Pixel (or simply Facebook Pixel) is a Javascript code that you can place on the backend of your website and allows you to monitor the actions of your audience in the hopes to optimize results. This is why it's important to install Facebook Pixel before launching your Facebook ads.

With Facebook Pixel, you're able to understand if an ad is working, what the ad's return on investment is, and what you can do the next time around to optimize better results. Facebook Pixels also directly tells you if your target audience has bought a product, added something to their cart, or looked through your online catalog. This is important when comparing what worked with what hasn't in your ads. In later chapters, we will discuss A/B Testing and implementing Facebook Pixels into your product page is imperative for this analysis to occur.

So how does it work? Well, each ad account on Facebook gets a default "pixel" to use.

Facebook Pixels are one singular code made of two parts: the base code and the event code. While the base code will track all the traffic on your side, the event code will allows you to track specific actions on those pages. This can seem a bit confusing at first, but any web designer with a basic understanding of Javascript coding will be able to implement this onto your website. Aside from that, Facebook give you codes that will help you get what you want out of your Facebook Pixel. For instance, if an online store owner wanted to see which visitors placed items in their cart, but didn't complete the purchase - they would add the event code to the backend of their website. This would allow them to run hyper-targeted ads to just these people.

Now that you're aware on what pixels are, it's time to install the code and use the platform strategically. First, open Facebook Ads Manger and select the top menu button. Then click Pixels, where you will be able to select Create a Pixel to begin the process. Here Facebook will allow you to give your latest Pixel a name. This can be any name. Once you have decided on one, select Next at the bottom right side of the screen.Now you will need to install the pixel.

This can be done by utilizing the Tag Manager Plugin or by manually copying and pasting the code in. Facebook also gives you the option to email the code to a web developer ti implement the service for you. But if you selected to copy and paste the code, you will be taken to the Install Pixel Base Code Page. Here you will click into the code box to copy the code and page it into the header tags of your website under the SEO settings. While every domain host is different, yours should specific instructions on how to paste into your header tags.

Our next step brings us to implementing the event code, which is installed to track actions taken on your website's pages. This is important when implementing A/B testing and understanding the behaviors of your audience when it comes to your ads. Here you will need to choose which event code you would like to track. Facebook gives you a myriad of options. Once you have made your decision on what you would like to track, select the event code and click in the code box to copy the code like once before. You will then be able to place this event code on the respective pages of your website. Please note that these implemented codes are only meant for the relevant pages of your website and will only work accordingly. You can then proceed to the next step by selecting Next.

Now you can test the pixel's status and see if the pixel has been installed correctly. It typically takes Facebook Pixels 30 minutes to be installed and updated properly. Once this is done, you will be able to access the Pixel data by going to Ads Manager. A graph will show how many times your pixel has been fired. For URL graphs, you will be able to see the popularity of a certain page over the last 14 days of your pixel activity. You can also see if most people are using mobile devices to click on your ads, which would be helpful in changing your Ads to only being based on mobile going forward.

Other strategies can be assessed from Facebook Pixels as you begin analyzing the data from the platform. This will give you a good idea on what is exactly working with your Facebook ads and how impactful tracking can be.

Chapter 7: What Facebook Ad Tools Should You Take Advantage of?

As Facebook Ads has taken over the advertising space for many companies, the social media platform has developed other tools to help marketers. From the Power Editor to allowing you to boost posts, Facebook Ads has allowed businesses to grow further than before.

Power Editor

Power Editor is a mass ads creator and management tool that is often used by larger advertisers on Facebook who want more features than what's traditionally offered through their ad platform. It's basically a plugin that works with different web browsers. Through this plugin, you're able to download all you data from the Ads Manager and create campaigns. You can then click Upload Changes to begin running those ads. Your advertisements will then be available to view through Ads Managers. But if any changes are needed to be made to features only in Power Editor, you will need to re-down your ads, you will have to re-download the ads, make your preferred adjustments, and upload them all over again. This is the only downfall to having this program. But being able to bulk create ads and manage them is worth having to start over again in the process.

Benefits of the Power Editor

Power Editor has a lot of other interesting features that makes the program standout from most Facebook Ad components. A major benefit is that the new features that are made live on Facebook for advertisers are shown first on the Power Editor.

Besides this, many advertisers love that they are able to budget and schedule their Ad Set area through Power Editor. This is key if you know what times of the day your audience is on Facebook. This can also be quite useful to improve ad metrics by presenting your ads at these times. You can also pick a time zone that your ad will run in, creating an even more hyper-targeting approach to the demographics of your audience.

The Power Editor can also be quite handy for an app developer because you can control the finite details of when your ad is shown. This includes being able to only show your ad on phones that are connected to WiFi. But besides this ability, you can also bulk upload onto the

Power Editor - which is what brings a lot of developers and marketers to the tool. With this feature, you can upload an Excel spreadsheet of your ads and download those to edit as well.

Optimization also seems to be of utmost important for most advertisers. Power Editor allows you to analyze all the same things you can do in Ads Manager. But instead of just looking at clicks or impressions - you can choose a daily reach that allows you to bid on impressions, but inherently limit the views to once a day. This kind of optimization will allow you to test different ad products and see what works best for your audience.

One of the best to use Power Editor is the Unpublished Post feature. An unpublished post is similar to a normal page post in that it has longer text, but it also includes a call-to-action button and you can control what the link looks like. Unpublished posts are useful because you can split test your ads without posting more than one time on a page. This means you're know posting too much promotional content for your fans. The trick is to post by using the + sign on your post and not try to update already published posts. You can have longer text in the post to tell people more about your offer when you utilize unpublished posts.

Videos

As mentioned before, video is often the best way to grow your brand or business. So, starting a Facebook page that features videos might be one of your goals since some brands receive high levels of engagement and revenues from the platform. It is also reported to be the number one platform where people find out information and tutorials. So, let's get started.

Pick a niche. What is your brand trying to say or accomplish on the platform? Are you attempting to create a personal touch with your business? This can be successfully conveyed by featuring behind-the-scenes videos or creating blogs with your staff. Whatever you decide your motive to be, be consistent and concise in building your videos around it. Remember that this is an extension of your brand, so make sure it contributes to the mission of your company.

Research Similar Brands. Now it's time to find and discover the types of videos that you want to create. From inspirational to informational, you can find what there is a demand for with your new Facebook Video account. You can also see what other creators are doing on the platform to engage with their followers. While we don't suggest copying, it is important to be aware what is successful on the platform and what is not. So becoming inspired by a similar brand shouldn't be an issue.

Create Videos. The great thing about marketing on Facebook Video is that the platform allows you to upload from any device. So depending on your budget, you can decide to invest in a high quality camera or use your high definition smart phone to record videos. The purpose is that you cultivate a following that follows and engages into the narrative of your brand.

Engage With Your Subscribers. It's also important to reply to any comments on any of your videos to connect with viewers and keep them connected to your brand.

Monetize Your Page. Although this step can't be done until you have over 1000 subscribers and 4000 watch hours in one year, it's important that you submit your application to become a Facebook Video Creator and properly monetized. This can also open up other exclusive features including doing post on your subscribers' feeds and live video. You will also be able to use any of the monetized money you receive to put back into your brand and other marketing campaigns.

Recently, video marketing's popularity has increased due to its conductibility with customers being better than other social networks. With this, there's also an increased competition over consumers' time and attention. But while a lot of Facebook Video videos are being posted daily, they don't all work. If you visited Facebook Video today and you would find well over a million of videos without comments and struggling to hit 5 views. Many advertisers haven't figured out how they can get more engagement on their Facebook Video platform. But there have been a couple of proven strategies that can help manage your Facebook Video and contribute to your over all Facebook Video analytics.

Shorter videos will often get more views. While you may receive less monetization for these videos, you will receive better engagement and response from your audience. A recent study showed that videos up to 2 minutes will get almost half of Facebook Video's views for the months. Simply put, videos that are less than two minutes are doing much better than those longer. This could have to do with people's attention span. It's also important to utilize Search Engine Optimization when optimizing your videos for Facebook Video. This will allow you to increase traffic through organic search traffic on Google and beyond. But with Facebook Video, search engine optimization can make your videos easier to find on Facebook Video search. This means the higher on user's search engines, the more views they'll likely get.

Now search engine optimization is different for each social media platform, but the key ideals will remain the same. Their tactical application just changes as different marketing pages have different requirements and rules. The three SEO tools that can help include keyword optimization, extending your video description past a couple of words, and just promoting your videos a lot on all your social medias.

- Keyword optimization. Look up keywords before posting a video to make sure that it ranks higher in what you're targeting. Also make sure that the keywords you are desiring to be targeted are getting high search volumes before including them in the title of your video.
- Use descriptions to have more SEO results. Facebook Video uses the text around your video to determine how it should be ranked in their search results, which is why the description and title is so important. You can keywords beyond the tags in the video descriptions to up the probability of receiving a higher ranking and inevitably getting more clicks to your video.

- Promote across all platforms once you upload a video. It can be daunting, but do to the competitive nature on Facebook Video, you will need actively promote your videos. Using other platforms like Facebook, Instagram, and Twitter can certainly help get your Facebook Video videos viewed by the right people for higher engagement.

This has been mentioned before, but it is so important to be consistent with posting quality content and also interacting with your audience as well. Your page just will not succeed if there is no audience to engage with. Posting quality content on a regular basis will keep audiences built in and looking for your next video. Remember that long periods of non-engagement on any social platform can essentially kill your page and engagement metrics. It's so important to be involved and not to stop posting frequently. You may even want o maintain a posting schedule so that fans and subscribers can look forward to your upcoming updates.

Besides your optimized marketing strategies, Facebook Video will provide you analytics that will help you grow your page. While the creative side of Facebook Video is very important, it's also important to analyze metrics and see what it is working on the platform as you have done for previous social media accounts. Often knowing how much time users spend on your videos, can influence the length of your video and amount of creativity you put into the video. This does not mean to slack on effort, but it is wise to understand your audience. If you're trying to sell frying pans, it may not be wise to post an expensive video glamorizing the life of a family who uses the product. Sure people will want to

Facebook Video Analytics can also tell you the average time your videos are played, the traffic sources like Facebook Video or Facebook that your videos come from, the demographic of viewers, and audience retention. This is different from the other platforms because you can get into the minutiae to see who watches your videos and why. It's always important to understand what drives your engagement. But at the end of the day, it's also important to understand patience when building any brand. You shouldn't expect a huge Facebook Video following off the bat. But share your videos, comment more, do more collaborations with similar brands to drive those following numbers. By doing this, you've began to analyze your Facebook Video page and can start promoting it to even more users because you've established your core demographic.

Chapter 8: How to Analyze Your Results

Analyzing Facebook results can be overwhelming for any advertiser. But by paying attention to the little details and being selective on the data you analyze, you can certainly use your ads to cultivate a successful ad audience.

Typically, when you focus on the smaller things in Facebook Ad Analytics, the biggest differences are made. These smaller things will lead to you being able to see trends across different variables. A key thing that you can do is name each of your ads a different variation that you're using. From 'Audience Gender' to 'Device Type,' this simple way of titling each of your ads can make all the difference when analyzing results. The added bonus is once you export and begin looking at your report, you'll be able to separate the Ad Name into individual columns. This will allow you to sort your data into segments and create tables for the individual segments. These visual trends will allow you to see how your current ad strategy is impacting the overall market and your direct audience.

It's also wise to understand that not all data that Facebook provides is worth your time analyzing. Your brand may benefit from some stats and not need to be influenced by others. Customize your Facebook Ads Manager columns to include only the important metrics for your ad campaign and arrange them in the order that makes the most sense to you. You can create custom columns on any ad set and ad level. You can also do this on any campaign level if you are running multiple campaigns. The columns you decide on featuring will obviously depend on your objectives and the most important metrics for your ad campaign. For instance, the goal of your many marketers' ads are to take action on your website. So one of the most important metrics on Facebook will be website conversions and cost-per-acquisition. You can also take a look at your ad video views and see how many people watched half (50%) or all (100%) of your video. And lastly, metrics like click-through-rate and completion rates will tell you helpful performance metrics for your ads. This is all available on the Facebook Ads Manager interface. You can save these custom column presents to access in the future.

Facebook Ad Manager's Breakdown function is another tool in allowing you to see performance across various segments. You won't even have to set up these segments within your ad sets. So if you can breakdown your campaign or ad set by gender, device, or gender. This can be helpful if you want to create different ads that test these newly set criteria, but still want to understand how age and gender can influence your ads.

In addition to the campaign metrics you see in your Ads Manager reports, you can take your Facebook ads reporting routine one step by using the Breakdown menu. By using the Breakdown menu, you can break down your campaign reports by:

- **Delivery**: This includes gender, age, gender, device, time of day, and location.
- **Action**: This includes destination on your website, video view type, carousel card, or conversion device,
- **Time**
  - You can elect to choose from one of the criteria listed above from each section (i.e. one from Delivery, one from Action, and one from Time) to create proper analyzation.
  - Using the campaign breakdown, you can find answers to many questions, including:

- What ad placement is delivering the best
- What times of the day has the most conversions at the lowest cost?
- Where are the best performing target countries?
  - o To break down these ad campaigns by different criteria, choose one or more Facebook campaigns. After, click a criteria from the Breakdown menu and you can begin comparing and analyzing.Lastly, there are some things that you can do even further to properly utilize these newly found results.
- **Pause lower performers**. If you ever recognize that video ads have higher conversion rates than single image ads for one user group, then you may want to pause this image for this group. This will not only help metrics, but will help you avoid alienating certain audiences.
- **Boost higher performers.** Try boosting the budget for your users achieving the lowest cost-per-result

and the most results. This will be based on your primary goal.

- **Add in new ad versions.** If your carousel ads are outperforming single image ads, you can choose to create an additional carousel ad testing out a new version or variation of what you tried before.
- **Modify your audiences**. This is simple. If one audience group is reacting to your ads more, then refine your demographics to that group without alienating others.
  - o The best practice to analyzing any ad is letting the data guide you to all your knowledge and future decision. With this in mind, you'll be able to build trust and loyalty with your audience as you begin to define your brand.

Chapter 9: How to Build Your Sales Funnel

Building a sale funnel is important to any Facebook ad since it improves conversions and builds an overall engagement from your audience. Traditionally, when advertisers create their Facebook ad, they often do it with the wrong goals in mind. With a campaign focused on conversion, you can set up multiple conversions that you can track and optimize for. You can also create custom conversions as mentioned before for your site. There could include viewing content, adding to cart, and purchasing. Advertisers will traditionally choose conversion objectives that don't at all lead to actual conversions. So while they may target having users fill out a contact form, the truth is that this conversion only happens a couple times of week. And having ads to have these users fill out a form could just lead to another casual, and sometimes cold audience member. Facebook often recommends that the conversion type you choose happens over 50 times a week per ad set that you choose. These numbers can actually lead to actual metrics. Many don't realize it so they pick something that doesn't happen to often based off of something they perceive to have a lot of conversions.

If you run a conversion campaign that doesn't have enough data, Facebook doesn't know how to optimize it. It's important to remember that Facebook Ads is based an algorithm. So if you have a niche audience one kind of person buying one kind of product, your cam pain can maybe work, but the conversions will be lower. Facebook needs 50 conversion to essentially see the behaviors of users and find other users like them to promote your ad to. Without that crucial data, Facebook is likely to struggle finding an audience. In order maximize this ad spend, change how you perceive conversions from your sales funnel.

The best conversion might be someone purchasing your product, but it's important to understand the steps the audience takes before that purchase. Remember this is the data that Facebook likes to analyze as well to target users who take similar steps. So your initial engagement goal might not be the conversion goal you're seeking, but the choices these users make in buying your product. This is a sales funnel.

If someone who sells an informational product wants customers to contribute to something more expensive course, people aren't going to give right away. They will like to so in increments, which may include signing up for a free guide, then enrolling in a paid for webinar, and then contribute to an expensive course. Users need to feel validated in trusting your brand before outright purchasing the product. By targeting an action that happens earlier in your sales funnel, you will cultivate data to find how to convert audiences in their infancy.

Now that you've found the right actions early on in your funnel, you can focus on your campaign. When you initially set up a campaign on Facebook Ads, it will immediately what you want to accomplish. And almost everyone wants a conversion since they are trying to sell something. But once you choose the conversion campaign type over reach, store visits, or even engagements, you're locked into that campaign type and all its offering. However, there are other campaign types that are more cost efficient and can lead to more conversions as well.

Video funnels tend to be the best type of funnel because it allows the product to be explained. The steps to asking for a purchase of your good and service can be done in one video and it introduces someone to the product quickly. Since Facebook has added customer audiences, more people can now be targeted and funneled much easier than before. So if you can retarget an audience based on how much of a video they've watched. you can reduce cost by refining your video to creating higher engagement. This inevitably saves money because you're focusing on the organic nature of selling to a client rather than basing it off of just getting a purchase. For a video campaign, Facebook usually charges you based on cost per one thousand impressions, which is a fraction of the cost for running a full-on conversion conversion campaign. This approach allows you to align the action with what the cost should be. A video views campaign can also help you reach a wider and different audience compared to one based on conversion. In order to understand this, you need to understand how the audience targeting for different campaign types works as well.

When you set up an audience targeting for your ad, the size of your audience will either increate or decreases based on the criteria you added or removed from it. But when you run an ad, it doesn't show up for all those people. A fraction of those people will see the advertisement because Facebook shows it only to those who are more likely to be converted. Those people will not be the same who are most likely to watch a video. This difference doesn't imply that people are likely to watch the video won't buy. The different is that the video views audience doesn't seem like the people are necessarily going to purchase your product any faster. But this is actually more important. You want an audience who is going to engage in your product at different phases rather than just click and buy it. Video-based campaigns can help you build this audience more organically than before.

Alternatively, since Messenger ads are conversation-based and create a personal connection, this may be important to create a successful sales funnel. If a user interacts in your ad in this way, this means that they are an engaged audience member. They care about the product enough to ask questions and engage with your team (or automated team) to inevitably learn more about your brand. This digital part of your sales funnel can do wonders for 'word-of-mouth' and garner an organic following that you hadn't expected previously. With Messenger Ads, an ad will appear on your news feed, but instead of a Shop Now Button immediately taking you to a website, it will have a Messenger icon on it. While this may not lead to the immediate metric of receiving a sale or having someone add to a cart, it will increase someone's trust in your brand and establish you a new customer. These objectives are much more important to a success of a new digital ad campaign than simply receiving a sale. Engaging with these remarketed individuals build lifelong loyalty and will establish your brand identity for years to come.

The Psychology of Building A Successful Sales Funnel

When advertisers begin to establish a funnel, it's important to dig into deciding Interests and Custom Audience. But they'll traditionally realize that they don't have any creative that will work for their funnel because what they've perceived to be successful is not. It's best to start with a content audit so that you can see what pieces of your ad works and what might be missing. An audit will also give you proper ideas for your ideal sales funnel to launch now rather than be created. In your audit, you should include any marketing tool that you have that's ready to be launched now including that blog post that received great feedback. After you've completed the audit, cut whatever hasn't worked or received great feedback. What hasn't led to a conversion in the past. Taking a step back in identifying what efforts have worked will allow you to move forward creative and use new tactics to target your audience. You also now know what kind of ad, blog, or marketing content you need to recreate to help gain more warm audience member. These disengaging or non-effective marketing tools that you have launched before can change warm audiences to told in a minute. This is why this audit is important in building a successful funnel.

Next, it's important to decide what ind of audiences you already have. Do you have a contact list? If so, how big is it? How much traffic does your website get from this. This data will be a good starting point for retargeting members. As mentioned before, you can also create a lookalike audience based on your contact list. But the observation we're getting at is that this inventory of your audience data is so important to continue establishing your funnel. Target interests of these members and begin building more audience members from there. Even adding another interest or layering to how you target audience can refine these results for a warmer audience.

After you understand what your audience has, you can start developing an idea for the different types of audience you will be dealing with. These are audience are called cold (top-of-funnel), warm, and hot audience (bottom-of-funnel). Cold audiences are users who have never visited your site or interacted with your brand in any type of way. Traditionally, you haven't served them an ad or video because you don't know what to offer them. Warm audiences are typically the engaged retargeted group. These are usually those who haven't visited your website, but are on your Customer List and have interacted with your ads. They're interested in your brand, but they haven't moved into actually committing to a purchased.

Warm audience members will often watch 25-50% of your ad video, which can give you an idea of how engaged they are. Similarly, hot audiences that are at the bottom of the funnel have been to your website. You can generally put extra parameters on these users to ensure that they are really engaged. For example, you can retarget these users by seeing who visited your site, but actually engaged in the products on the landing page.

Once you decide what users belong to which funnel type (cold, warm, or hot), you can revisit you content to see what makes sense to your different audience. Content for the bottom of the funnel will typically be focused on selling since this audience often know your brand and what you can offer. You can typically show this audience something that explains what your brand does in specific detail since they are already engaged. Sure, your new ad content may seem more salesy and dense, but remember this audience already knows you so it won't feel that way. You'll only be providing them more information, which may lead to more engagement and these members becoming unofficial ambassadors of your brand. Adversely for a cold audience, you'll definitely want to share something that won't take much time or effort for the intended user. A blog post or video can typically provide information and engage top of the funnel audiences without alienating them.

At this point, you're ready to set up ads and track who takes action and how these users move through your sales funnel. The objective in building any sales funnel is moving one audience to the next down your funnel. So while it's still imperative to create ads for the cold audience at the top of the funnel, it's also important to create ads that moves those users into the warm audience. While users in the warm audience are still important, if your content is substance-less text instead of a video, it may be difficult to. Facebook will allow you to create custom audience by choosing the video people watched, but doesn't let you to create a custom audience based on other content types. That's why a video is often better to track engagement on than other posts.

Regardless of how you move your users from the top of the funnel to the bottom, it is important to do so at all times. It's very easy for marketers to get caught up in pleasing the cold or warm audiences without realizing that they want to secure their loyalty at different levels of consideration. This will not only benefit your metrics and make it cheaper for you to advertise, but will build the longevity of your business as users will want to interact with your ads more and more. And once you start introducing remarketing to your already engaged users, you'll see the payoff sooner than ever.

Chapter 10: How to Set Up Remarketing

Once you have successfully set up your ads and sales funnel, you are ready to introduce your targeted audiences to remarketing. While many only users believe the ads they see is divinity or fate, they've often just been a target of remarketing. Remarketing is when algorithms follow the behaviors of user from around the internet to present a related offer. If a user visits your website, they are usually tagged by those web "cookies" that people traditionally don't see a reason for. Well, for advertisers - they are keep to building an audience. When you remarked to visitors of your website, a code is enabled on the webpage that a user visits, and this triggers your ads to follow those user around the internet. From social media websites to the advert banners on random websites, these cookies users will be targeted with your ads.

Remarketing isn't anything new on the internet as many brands have found ways of using users online behaviors to bring them back to their sites. Google Ads even allows marketers to remarked by creating lists with a rule set. Advertisers can choose to target all website visitors, those to a specific page, or single out the ones who have completed a special action of your choose. Google will then enable ads to show the same visitors on sites on their Display Network. Facebook's remarketing program is very similar.

Instead of remarking to those on other websites across the web, Facebook's remarketing is showing ads solely on Facebook. the site will commonly refer to these users who are being remarketed towards as 'Custom Audiences.' The idea is the same as mentioned before: once someone interacts with your site or visits, they are tracked with a code to follow their behavior online. Once this user visits their Facebook feed, the code signifies the ad to show up while they are scrolling and remind the user what they are missing. This can be done one of three ways: Website Traffic (the most popular), Customer List, or App Activity. These type of remarketing will be listed under Create a Customer Audience when you are ready to start remarketing your audience.

Website Traffic

This is type of remarketing is the most popular because it's the most typical use of the strategy. It will serve adverts to those who have gone to your website within a specified time frame. And if you've initiated Facebook Pixels on all pages of your website, you can target specific audience through filters. This will based on the pages they've gone to. For example, if you are selling athletic gear and want to target those searching for athletic shorts, you can set up an audience that elicits ads to just people who visited pages with shorts in the web URL.

Customer List

This is perhaps the most effective tool on Facebook because it allows you to serve personalized ads to a list of customer contact that you've already received. With these lists, Facebook can be more like email marketing to targeted people with personalized messages. Talk about hyper-targeting your market. From phone numbers to email addresses to even unique user IDs, you can find a list of contacts, upload it into Facebook and target them with ads.

App Activity

App activity is a way to show a specific group of people relevant ads based on their behaviors. So if someone abandons their online shopping cart, you can target them with the same product at a discount. You can even directly target users who have used your app before and build a rapport with them. While creating these direct and personalized messages can be timely, they can often lead to a sell or a wanted impression for your data.

To get started with remarketing, click into your Facebook Ads Manager and select the Tools dropdown and click Audiences. After, click on Create Audiences and Custom Audiences from the choices provided. Here you will be able to choose exactly what remarketing list you would like to create from and what type of audience you would like to create. These are the same ones that have been listed previously including Website Traffic, Customer List, and App Activity.

Under Customer List, you will be able to import a list by comping and pasting a customer list of emails and contact information or uploading a text file. Please note that this file can only be .txt. or .csv. Facebook also allows you to integrate your customer list through MailChimp and upload this way. Once this is done, you can select Create Audience.

Now if you would like target Website Traffic, you will need to install your Facebook Pixels on each page of your site.If you've already installed a Custom Audience Pixel as suggested in Facebook Pixels Chapter, you can skip this step.

Since every ad account is only allowed one Facebook Pixel to remarked users, this step can only be done once. But to do so, select the Tools dropdown menu at the top of the webpage. Choose Pixel, then Create A Pixel, and name your pixel. Once you've created your pixel, be sure to place it in the <head> tags of every page of your site. Then, you'll return to the Create a Custom Audience page and choose Website Traffic. Here you can choose the parameters the visitor has to meet in order to be remarketed. For example, for anyone who just visited your site or page that contains the word "boots" in the URL. Name this audience (like: "Boot Shoppers," "All Visitors." "Visited Lead Pages"), and create the page. After this, you can either create ad sets that you can tie into your consumer audience or apply them to ad sets you've already created. This will establish your Facebook Ads to be officially remarketed to your consumers on Facebook.

Since you now understand the power of remarketing on Facebook, we've gathered some other tips that may help you strategize better than your competition.

Every Facebook pages first goal is to get as many Facebook page likes as possible - organically, of course. It can be tricky gaining these followers authentically as you are a new company in the space. But fortunately, Facebook allows you to run campaigns with the main purpose to get page promoters. While this may seem like buying followers at first, since it's through remarketing you're really just reaching fans who are already engaged in your product. This can leader to even higher engagement, organic visibility through sharing, cheaper clicks for your business, and higher relevancy metrics with your audience.

Now if you have advertised previously with Google Ads, you're likely cognizant of how your Quality Score can affect the way your ad is ranked and the price you pay per click. Similarly, Facebook has a metric called relevance score that tells you how much you pay and how frequently your ad is shown to your target audience. The engagement rates affect this relevance score, which will much higher if you're showing your ads to warm audiences of your brand. You want your audience to be brand ambassadors who are going to engage in your ads so that every post has a high relevance score, which will inevitably lead to more visibility and cheaper click. This is the best way to your page. By focusing on the people who are already familiar with your brand and champion of your products through remarking. There's also a bonus in the authenticity of engaging with actual fans of your brand. They're likely to 'like' your posts or page and then it shows up in their social circles on the website. This can organically lead to more followers that you hadn't intended to connect with before.

With these new followers, it's imperative to make sure that they see and engage in your remarketed ads and posts. You can even take the focus of "buying these remarketed followers" one step further by boosting posts these same Facebook followers. This is a great tactic in increasing visibility even further since these individuals have already loyal to the brand and will most likely want to inevitably aid the cause of bettering your metrics. This will once again lead to an organic reach and even higher relevance scores on the platform.

You could also layer your custom audience with Facebook's hyper-targeting options.If you understand your target audience well enough, you'll have no problem finding them. The amount of granularity that you can have with Facebook targeting option is astonishing. While it's important to not get too limited and finite in your reach for a new audience, you also want to stay faithful to your brand. Becoming follower hungry and stretching beyond the bounds of your target audience to every Facebook user on the planet actually leads to less visibility, less profitability, and even lower relevance scores. This is why it's important to know your audience and understand who exactly you're targeting or you could waste your budget on a cold audience who wants no part in your brand.

So let's say you've uploaded over a thousand contracts via your Customer List and only have $200 to spend. Instead of using a dollar of your budget here and there, you would be better off combining your customer list with a targeted demographic that is ready to buy your product or service. Generally, the goal is to find the perfect balance between budget and audience size, but also extending your options by targeting new users within the walls of a proven audience who has taken to your brand.

It's also wise to not overextend your brand onto your remarketed audience by fatiguing them with the same propaganda over and over again. The lifespan of a Facebook ad is generally short and if your target audience sees the ad too much, they may be over your brand. It's important to not run your ad into the ground by having it continuously appearing until the budget runs out. So if your ad features a sale or special offer, it may be a good idea to focus this limited time during a season where people are more likely to buy your product like before the holidays. You can run the ad aggressively during this time without frequency caps and to a remarketing list that may be looking for your product but didn't end up purchasing before.

Now if you just want to promote your page to website visits, you might try an on-going ad set where you can change the ad from time to time to keep it fresh. You can also set up schedules so that you ad is on a specified schedule for days of the week rather than being active all week long. If you notice higher traffic and conversion metrics happening during certain hours, it would be wise to schedule your ads accordingly. This is a great way to captivate and engage in audiences selectively. It also allows you to save your budget and deploy your ads during times where it can be best used.

Lastly, layering lookalike audiences onto custom audiences will allow you to expand your reach to entirely new set of leads. You will also find an untapped audience by doing this. But it's highly effect because all you're basically doing is cloning your remarketing list and finding a group of unknowns. The great thing about essentially cloning your custom audience is that you know those users are"in-market" and can easily and most likely be converted to new fans of your company. The best thing from all of these strategies is that you're building a similar audience that you inherently already know the behaviors of. This is the goal of any marketer.

Chapter 11: How to Master Ad Targeting

With Facebook having hundreds of hyper-targeting and ad demographic options, you can truly master ad targeting on the platform and zero-in on your target audience. From location to partner connections, you can target almost anyone based on anything as listed below.

- Location: You can target users by state, country or zip code. You can even get more specific too by targeting where users work versus where they live.
- Demographics: Demographics is data that relates to age, sex, income, marital status, and more. Facebook offers a ton of demographic options.
- Interests: Interests are simply the things that people enjoy and can be imperative to identifying a target market.
- Behaviors: Behaviors use the Facebook Pixel (discussed below) to target users.
- Engagement: Engagement is anytime a user comments, likes or follows you or your pages. If someone has recently likes a post,

you can target them on Facebook and show them your ads.

As mentioned in the chapter on Pixels, Facebook Pixels are a god-send when it comes to mastering ad targeting. The unique codes that are meant for the backend of your website will track behaviors on your web site and target visitors based on their behavior. The goal is obviously to optimize your Facebook Ads and collect as much data about its users. But it's also important to note that the analyzation of this data is even more crucial in building a successful audience on Facebook. Building this audience can take sometime because while you want your brand's audience to be specific, you don't want them to be niche. Traditionally when using Facebook Ads, you're not looking to build a business that only caters to a select few, but to build one that is accessible to all demographics.

The first move to creating this specific though broad audience is to understand your consumer base. You can even build a customer avatar to help set up a successful Facebook Audience. This is often taught during marketing courses in college, so that you can begin personifying the groups that you are seeking to attract. To build a customer avatar, begin with giving your customer an age, location, and gender. Then proceed with his/her goals and values, challengers and pain points, sources of information, and intentions for purchasing or buying into a successful business. These traits will give ups a great idea on the type of audience you want to garner support and attention from online.

Now that you have an idea for your desired audience, you should set up a saved audience on Facebook. A Facebook saved audience is an audience that you can create, save, and then use again for future campaigns. If you understand your target audience and demographic pretty well, you can use the info to create an audience that you can reuse for other ads later. To set up a saved audience, go to the Audiences page. Select Create A Saved Audience. Next you'll see the Facebook Ads Manager audience creation page. Here is where you start to plug in your preferred demographics that you found earlier when deciding on your costumers persona. When you've finally decided on location, interests, and demographics, you can select Create Audience. This new audience will appear on your Audiences pages. So now whenever you want to deploy this saved audience for future campaigns, go to the Audience tab on the left hand side and choose the audience you'd like to use.

Besides saved audiences, you can also create custom real-life audiences that you've had previous real world connections with. By uploading a list of emails or phone numbers, you can show your ads to a number of prospects under this tab. You can also have Facebook not show emails or numbers (i.e. if you have a list of people you know wont be interested with your service or products). Custom audiences can also work with Facebook Pixels to help show ads to individuals who have visited or interacted with your website.

To create a custom audience, go to the Audience page and click Create Audience and then select Create Custom Audience. Now you will see a page with Custom Audience options. If you have a list of emails or numbers, select Customer File. This will allow you to upload date from a file of your own or MailChimp - which is partnered with Facebook for custom audiences. If using your own file, it's important to ensure that the film is a .CSV file or .TXT file for readability. Once you've uploaded the data, agreed to Facebook's Terms and Conditions, and named your audience - you can click Next.

Facebook will then provide a preview of your data and allow you to map your identifiers. So make sure that the information under Email are email addresses and not phone numbers. Facebook is known to automatically change the data. Your Custom Audience will now show up in your Audience list. As your data is still being uploaded, it will show Updating Audience with a blue dot next to it in the Availability column. Once you see that dot change to green and show Ready, then you will be ready to utilize it in running campaigns. Just remember that it's important to be specific, but not too niche when creating any of your Custom Audience. The results will be better, the broader the details are.

The last type of audience that can be created is a Lookalike Audience that targets users similar to the one in your Custom Audience, but maybe under a different demographic. So let's say you have a Custom Audience already set up, your Lookalike Audience could target a similar audience in another state. Even if the Lookalike audience isn't apart of the email or phone list that you uploaded, Facebook will find audiences similar on other criteria you've listed. To enable this, go back to Audience page, select Create Audience, and then Lookalike Audience.. Now you'll have an option to choose the Custom or Saved Audience that you would like to predicate your new lookalike audience one. Once you've decided on the basis of your Lookalike Audience, toggle settings for Location and Size and Create Audience at the bottom right of the screen. Here you will be able to compare audiences based on ad setups that you have had previously and target your ads more precisely than ever before.

The Custom Audiences tool can give marketers lots of options for refining their ad results and there's even more that can be done with targeting Website Traffic and Events. Custom Audiences also allows marketers to retarget people who have already visited your website, which can make the money you've spent on your ad go further. Studies have already shown that retargeted ads work more than the non-targeted ones. The average click through rate for a normal ad display is .07%, while one for a retargeted ad is .7%. This means that users are 164% more likely to click retargeted ads than non-retargeted ones; continuing to show that Custom Audiences and testing those audiences works.

If you want to get even greater success with mastering ads, target visitors who didn't complete a purchase. This can be done by using Pixel's traffic events. By creating an event attached to your product page's URL, then exclude any other URLs like the Completed Purchase page. So select a Create a Custom Audience from the Events Managers page and then drop down and choose People who visited specific webpage. Here you can choose how recent viewers should be for your ad by entering the number of days. Then, enter your product page's URL. This setup will advertise to only those who have visited your website in the past 30 days. You can even refine more by adjusting the frequency and device type respectively. But by the end of your adjustments, you will have hyper-targeted on an audience who usually doesn't follow through with purchases. This new re-targeting strategy could see a higher follow-through in purchases, especially if your re-targeted ad provides a discount of incentive that wasn't there before.

In conclusion, there are endless routes for you to utilize targeting on Facebook and master the art of the Facebook ad. Lookalike and Custom Audiences can help you get better follow-through rates by retarding and showing ads that are similar to the ones that convert most audience. By utilizing these tools, your test subjects will be even more inclined to purchase your products after you've refined your marketing tactics behind the scenes with targeted tests and deployment.

Chapter 12: What is A/B Testing and How do You Use It?

When the Internet was first invented, direct mail marketers would test a campaign with a small contingent of their contact list before committing to a full-blown campaign that could cost sometimes millions in printing and mailing adverts to customers. This would provide marketers the opportunity to preview their campaign launch in advance. Unfortunately, then, it was a very time-consuming process as marketing firms often had to begin testing their campaign months before their desired launch. Today, social media and Facebook has allowed this kind of testing to happen in real time. This is called A/B Testing.

Simply put, A/B testing is a type of research that allows you to try small changes in marketing to determine what is most effective with your targeted audience. Often known as split testing, A/B testing allows marketers to separate an audience into two groups and display a variation to each item. You will then compare the response to the different variations you provide and choose what is the best based on your metrics and preferences. The secret in having success in these tests is doing only one variation at a time. This can be an effective way to test your Facebook Ads to see what's most effective in how you deploy your ads.

A/B testing allows you to overtime refine your social media strategy and securing a winning formula for yourself. With Facebook Ads, many marketing mavens will test the actual text in the post. Typically, this can include the length of the post, use of emojis or punctuation, or even tone. This allows you to see the type of audience that will interact with the actual ad leading to a site visit or sale, or presents no engagement at all. You can also test the call-to-action that is featured in your ad. It's important that you customize the language to the one featured in your campaign. You wouldn't believe how much "Visit Our Site" vs. "Get Started" as clickable links influences audiences to interact. It also heavily depends on your brand and the audience that you are trying to connect to. While younger audiences may be attracted to adverts that are more indirect (i.e. 'Get Started' actually leading to your web page), older audiences will want to know what happens when they interact with the ad (i.e. "Visit Our Site" means exactly that). It just depends on what you are trying to convey.

Hashtags are also a great way to utilize A/B Testing because you're able to see if they are effective in extending reach. Once again, this is all based on your audience and you won't know if you test it on them. Pictures, gifs, and videos are another anomaly that can be tested against different audiences. While Internet marketers suggests that posts do better when there is a quirky gif attached, will this work for your company? This is why it's important to understand the culture of your brand or company before starting a new Facebook campaign. Even down to the ad format. You won't believe how many Facebook users actually want to see more of the product you are advertising before clicking and being taken to a third-party website. So maybe it's best to utilize a carousel ad or one that features multiple photos and videos. You wont know until you decide to utilize A/B Testing, which is why the method is used by so many marketers.

Running An A/B Test on Facebook Ads

First off, it's important to reiterate that it is of the utmost importance to test a small variation in your Facebook Ad at a time. If multiple variations are made at once, you unfortunately will be unable to understand why your ad engagement is increasing or becoming a success. Fortunately, social media has been a leader in making this kind of testing easier and much more efficient than the mail room days. Now you are ready to start the process in A/B Testing your Facebook Ads.

Once you choose an variable to test, it is very important to understand why you are choosing this variable. Remember that it is best to make this small change based on what you have already perceived to make the interaction better with the consumer. Maybe you've seen that individuals aren't interacting with the ad much since there are too many words and a video associated (which is already taking up their time). If you replace the video with a photo, and see better results, then you can move onto shortening the text in your ad. If audiences are engaging more, this means that the previous iteration of the ad was too wordy and time consuming. Trust your gut and research in taking on this step. Because once you choose a small variation, know that it will take some time to assess and analyze why it is working.

After choosing two variations, it's important to track and analyze this. You will then be able to choose which variation did better and make this variation or change available to all audiences that your ad reaches. It's also wise to document these changes in a separate log or journal as A/B Testing never quite ends as you are continually making changes to increase engagement. But by running these steps time and time again, you will find an audience who is receptive of what you are offering.

Chapter 13: How to Scale Your Facebook Ads

With any new business objective - being marketing or otherwise, you tend to want to explore other ways to growing your business even further. Scaling your Facebook Ads are no different, especially if you are looking to increase the size of your warm audience. These are consumers who interact with ads and end up purchasing on your website. Scaling these advertisements to them increases your advertisement spending while maintaining a positive return, but this can be difficult for any business. But by increasing audience size, building an effective funnel, and increasing your budget, increasing the impact your Facebook ads can become a success.

Increasing Your Audience Size

Moving from a small, tight audience to a broader, larger one will provide your Pixels more opportunities to find new consumers. You can often start by expanding lookalike audiences. A 1% lookalike audience based on a list of customers is where many advertisers will begin their hyper-targeting strategies. But after some time, ad performance may slow down as a large part of your audience will have already seen your ad. Some signs that you might be reaching a breaking point with audiences can include increased CPMs, a drop in overall performance, and higher frequency rates.

Although 1% Lookalike Audience includes some of the best prospects to compare again, if you were to expand to 3% or 5% audience size - you would be able to scale your budget without irritating your audience. An expansion to this audience size will typically consist of 5-10 million new customers to run trial against. You will also find that secondary markets is a strategic way to reach new costumers at a lower cost.

Building Your Funnel

Many new advertisers will set up their initial campaigns to find more costumers or retarget their website visitors. But it may be wise to focus on building a warm audience that consists of users who have some interest in your brand. We've mentioned before that it is better to focus on consumers who may actually be interested in what your company has to offer rather than social engagement via likes. It's also cheaper to target interested audience members rather than not. So by taking a portion of your marketing budget and redistributing it to higher funnel objectives, you will cultivate a larger warm audience that cane retargeted for purchases. High funnel objectives are video views, clicks, add to cart, initiate checkout, or overall content views. They are actionable things that can verify direct evidence that an ad is working.

As you begin to scale your ads to more people, your audience size will organically become much larger. So you may want to begin segmenting groups in order to find who has the highest returns. If you don't begin segmenting these retargeted audience, your budget could be going to the lower performing group like site visitors, when it is actually those who Add to Cart without purchasing who could benefit from your budget more.

Increasing Your Budget

Increasing your budget is the most natural step in scaling your ads. No matter if you decide to set up a daily, weekly, or monthly budget, scaling Facebook Ads means putting more money into the program to drive further results. Of course, spending more on marketing without evidence of a return can scare any business owner. But by listening to the data and Facebook's principles on how to set your budget, you can certainly spend your money more wisely. But once again, pay attention to the 'learning phase.' This can often give you guidelines to how much budget you should put into a new campaign or ad set.

You can now also run split tests with your campaign in order to optimize budgets. With this new feature, you can set a large budget upfront and let your various audiences compete for that budget. Facebook will recognize which ad set is most profitable and shifty out budget towards that campaign or ad set. To do this, toggle over Create Split Test to identify the best optimization strategies. These tests will also give you the ability to scale your daily budget without wasting it on an audience that doesn't follow through on purchases or other wanted metrics.

Develop New Creative Objectives

If you want to scale your Facebook ads, it's equally important to scale the creative side of your ads as well. While running multiple ads is a smart way to reduce creative fatigue, it's better to have your ads speak to customers at different levels of considerations. For instance, having a video introducing users to your business can certainly work at first. Especially to a cold audience because it allows you to see who watched fractions of your video even if they didn't click through to your website. This is your captivated audience of high performers. Now you can use this information to service a wide variety of formats to these prospects at this stage in your funnel. You could add testimonials or answer questions within your ad to move this warm audience to the purchasing phase of your product.

Other ways you can encourage the bottom of your funnel (casual website visitors, those who don't commit to purchases, etc.) is by presenting discounts and coupon cones in your Facebook Ads. By changing your ad at the consideration stage, you can engage an audience that would have traditionally not bought goods and influence them to complete their purchases.

Many marketers also overlook their previous customers for targeting since ads are traditionally attempting to garner a new audience. Utilizing Catalogue Sales or Dynamic Product Ads will solely show your consumer products they might be interested in purchasing during their next cart session. Also, if you have an excess of similar products, marketing these offering to your existing customers could be good incentive and contribute to your overall return on ad spending.

Now that you've introduced new ads to your Facebook funnel, you can optimize for multiple placements. If your ad only looks good on one of Facebook's platforms, you could miss out reaching a valuable customer on another. So when creating your campaign, you are given the option to Select all placements that support asset customization. When you initially create your ad, you will be able to choose the Facebook page and Instagram account you want your ad to run for. If you are operating a single ad image on Facebook under the standard ratio and it's doing well, you'll want to create one that is optimal for Instagram. At the Ad Set level, Facebook will allow you to upload multiple versions of your picture for different platforms. By doing this, Facebook will allow you to show your ads to new audiences across all its devices and platforms. This will decrease your click per impressions by allowing your ads to run in less competitive places on the platform.

The takeaway from scaling your ads is to take risk when it comes to analyzing what works and what doesn't for your ads. It's important to continuing running tests and apply these ads to different groups in order to see what will be the most successful. In doing this, you'll feel much more confident about how you spend your Facebook advertising budget going forward.

Chapter 14: How to Troubleshoot Facebook Ad Issues

So you've learned how to captivate a chunk of Facebook's 2 billion worldwide users on its adverting system? You've created test audiences, installed Pixels, and have your Business Manager up and running, but for some reason your ads aren't engaging with consumers the way you imagined. Well, there's nothing that a little troubleshooting can't fix.

Facebook Ads are often supposed to be an advertiser's wildest dream with a large database of people to tap into and the ability to segment and stack audience based not only on demographics, but also behaviors and preferences. But as mentioned in earlier chapters, your biggest downfall could be your audience selection. Whenever an audience selection is too narrow, you can often exhaust your segment way too quickly and drive up the cost per click of your ad. You could also neglect key consumers by narrowing the location and demo too much. Adversely, if your audience selection is too broad, you aren't really selling your ad to the people who may be interested in the first place. You could drive up the cost per click by providing poor audience matches or risk paying for clicks that won't end up being purchases by your costumers. It's an unfortunate game of finding the right balance in targeting your ads to the right individuals.

The solution is adding "and" to the detailed targeting section and widening your net if the audience selection is too narrow for your product or service. You can also utilize "and" to tighten up the your audience section. For instance, by choosing a field of study like History under Detailed Targeting, but making it also match with something that it normally wouldn't be linked with like Humor. This teaming may seem ridiculous at first glance, but for a comedy troupe that focuses on historical events - it may be the kind of hyper-targeting they need.

Another reason your ads may not be working is because your funnel is either too long or short. When someone clicks your ad, do users have to go through a sequence of pages before a conversion or tracked point takes place? If your funnel's too long and you put too many clicks between your initial click-through and the conversion event, you will most likely lose visitors. On the other side, if your funnel's too short, you can jar a user's experience with your business. An example of this would be asking for a sale immediately after they click on your ad. Consumers like to have time to think about their purchase, even if they are currently on the path to committing to that sale. Unfortunately, there's no troubleshooting for this event except to just understand your brand and its relationship with its consumer. Just make sure you build trust, awareness, and understanding between the path of your ad to asking for a sale for your customer.

Continuing, a big mistake marketers make in understanding their audience is creating a generic and broad ad that doesn't leverage any of the research or data behind the analytics that Facebook Ads has provided. This can be fixed by experimenting with clear objectives in your ad based on an audience segment's interests, purchasing behavior, and more. If just one segment consists of football fans according to your research, then a football analogy may seal the deal for the success to your ad and lead to better conversion.

Moreover, as the messages in an ad can be too broad and generic, they can also be mismatched and disconnected to your brand. You need to create a user experiences in your ad that matches those linked to the landing page or website that you are advertising. Too often are marketers focused on getting visitors to their homepage, but not selling them on the actual product. This is even more a problem if your analytics is based on a Pixel or conversion code that is on the Checkout page of your website. If a visitor can't see a product that they are offered in the ad, they will likely click off your landing page immediately. It's important that once users click on your ad, they are immediately able to identify what they are being offered.

A poor creative strategy and too much text in a image could be the problem as well. Facebook has been known to underserve an ad if there's too much text in the image that you have featured. This could even include your logo. And sure your ad was approved, but Facebook's algorithm tends to favor ads that feature little to no words in the actual picture of your ad. Facebook also favors ads that doesn't include its own logo. According to past studies and experiences, the platform tends to promote holistically original and non-manipulative ads to ones that try to evoke a click-through by piggybacking off their brand. To avoid this, just make sure to take heed to Facebook's initial warning when you upload your ad. Make the suggested adjustments in order to not be penalized. You can also attempt to try other formats if you still want to include text in your photos. Try the carousel format for example, where you will be able to incorporate multiple descriptions for different images. Facebook also had a Ad Overlay Checker Tool that you can use at any time to make sure your ad meets its requirements.

In earlier chapters, we spoke in-depth about having goals and objectives. Well, choosing the wrong objective in the beginning could lead to disappointment if your ad is not successful. For example, many marketers put value in getting the most likes for their page as possible. But many times this doesn't lead to conversions or click-through to the sites product page. This is because many users who "like" a Facebook page thanks to a snazzy ad won't actually be converted to paying customers. A business could also be so cool, trendy, and enticing, but most would never by the product because it's not for them. Marketers who run campaigns to get page likes will rarely receive actual sales from them. In the early 2010s, there was a trend where advertisers would present popular memes and gifs as ads that they would hope linked back to the consumers purchasing their product. But they never did. Alternatively, when Hulu used this strategy to run ads of funny clips from Family Guy (a show that would be shown exclusively on their new online service), subscriptions went through the roof. It's very important that the product you are presenting is the product you are selling because likes will not convert to any actual metric.

Lastly, it's very important that you continue monitoring your campaign segments even after you've started running ads.What you may have assumed about a performance on a mobile device, will likely not be the same on desktop. If this is ever the case, you always exclude poorly performing ads on Desktop by editing the Ad Set. Simply select Manage Placements and choose which devices you'd like to have your ads show on. This can improve your conversion data and make you feel more secure about your investments in the ad space. Moreover, continue monitoring your demographic breakdowns. If a demographic is not taking to your ad, either choose to exclude them from viewing your ad or run continual test to identify what works with them. You can always compare and contrast the different segments of your ads by going under any Campaign View and looking under the Breakdown tab.

If you have any other errors, Facebook Ads has a troubleshooting page that can assist you further. But if you continue to not have the luck with ads, always remember that there is no one size fits all answer to your Facebook Ad campaign. Achieving the highest click-through rate with the lowest cost-per-click is the obvious goal. It will take continual trial and error to optimizing the best ad performance for your current spend amount. Your ad performance can even fluctuate significantly for a short period of time after you have it go live. This is often called the learning phase.

Chapter 15: Understanding the Learning Phase

The learning phase is the time Facebook's algorithm takes to generate the best results for an ad campaign. This is typically right after an ad campaign is launched. This is often due to the fact that Facebook is presenting your ad to different combinations of people within your target audience, and then analyzing who took decisive action after your ads. Traditionally, new marketers will have a rough time introducing their new ads because Facebook is trying to find what audience will most likely click into their ad to make a purchase. Facebook has deemed this experimental phase the learning phase in order to optimize campaigns and increase their efforts for hyper-targeting.

The learning phase can also influence how you would to proceed with your campaign. If it takes Facebook longer to find an optimal audience for your campaign, it may be wise to make some slight changes to improve its performance. After all, you could be losing money if the campaign that you have set up doesn't provide a successful result during this "trial run." But if Facebook is able to find an optimal audience quickly, you may want to increase the budget of your campaign in order to captivate more consumers. This is why it's important to always keep a close eye on the results of your campaigns, especially at the beginning. It's just best to understand that you may find subpar results out of the gate.

So when does the learning phase commence?

The learning phase will start when you have launched your new Facebook ad campaign or made a major adjustment to a current campaign. Fortunately, Facebook tracks the learning phase progress and runs until your ad gets about 50 optimization events. Optimization events are chosen campaign objectives tested. So if you optimized your new ad to increase traffic, then the learning phase will proceed until it has approximately 50 link clicks. At this point, the learning phase ends and your campaign starts to run normal with improved results.

You can view the progress of the learning phase in the Delivery Column of the Ads Manager.

It's also important to understand that all learning phases are different. If you've elected for a Conversion objection and your window is a 7-day click, then the learning phase won't be finished until 50 conversions happen within 7 days of the user clicking the ad. This can set a longer time for the conversion window. And this time can be increased more if you are promoting a service or luxury product that requires longer deliberation times.

While rare, Facebook could remove your ad set form the learning phase if it fails to register 50 optimization events over a prolonged period of time. This means quite frankly that the ad was unsuccessful. It also means that your ad was too rare to meet any intended minimum targets. It may also mean that your ad isn't competitive enough to auction. Once again, it's wise to see the learning phase as a period in which you can analyze how well your ad may do. If your ad needs significant improvements in order to succeed with competition, this may be the best time to identify this. But just don't make any changes or edits during the actual learning phase itself.

Although best to take note of changes that you may make to a campaign in the future, making changes during a learning phase could delay any results and reset any useful data. Facebook needs the time to generate relevant data that will be useful in the future to give your ad campaign the motivation that it needs.

A learning phase will only be reset if you make a significant change to your campaign. This includes any targeting changes, changing an ad's creation, changing optimization event, or adding a new ad to your ad set. Pausing your ad set for 7 days or longer will also reset the learning phase. This just wont be done until you resume the paused ad set or campaign, causing even more of a delay. On the flip side, insignificant changes would include the increase or decrease budget amount or big cap/target cost amounts. To avoid a reset, just keep these changes on the lower end and you'll be right on your way to completing your learning phase and receiving the necessary data to analyze.

Chapter 16: What is Facebook's Attribution Window?

As Facebook users continue to interact with your ads, they will typically take part in a variety of action from visiting your website to watching your video. These actions are recorded, and Facebook will then report the action in Ads Manager. This is another tool that can be critical when determining how well your ads are doing, especially if you are running trials similar to A/B Testing. The attribution window is the number of days between when someone viewed or clicked on your ad and then took action on your website (like a visit or a purchase).

Since we have an understanding for how attributing works, it's now important to see how this conversion tracking works with Facebook Pixel that you've set up previously. If you have not installed Facebook Pixel already, it's important to do so in order to properly utilize Facebook's Attribution Window. Remember that the code that is added to your website allows Facebook to track when certain actions occur. The great thing about Facebook is that they allow you to choose from a number events to track. On the Install Pixel Code page, you will see a list of events that you can track with the most common being Viewed Content, Purchase, Add to Cart, and Initiate Checkout. Once you check the types of event codes you would like for Facebook to generate, you can then copy and paste the code into the backend of your website.

While this was already covered, it's wise re-iterate that you can that the number of Facebook Pixels pings matches with what has been reported in your conversion tracking. You can do this by opening Business Manager, select Ads Manager from the drop-down menu in the top left corner, and then choose Pixels under the Measure & Report section. Here you can see all the added data for each event pixel (i.e. Add to Cart, Purchase, Page Views, etc.) that you have set up. So, you can compare your actual number of page views to the ones reported on the attribution model. If you're still having issues with your pixels matching the data on your end, you can always launch the Pixel Helper Tool to see why your Pixels aren't reporting correctly. While you can change the settings, the default attribution window setting will show actions by users within their first day of seeing your ad to 28 days of clicking your ad. Settings can be changed for both the view and action window to 1, 7, or 28 days.

Considering what type of brand or business you have is important to deciding the time frame of your Facebook attribution weekend. For example, decisions that may take a longer time to make will need a longer window. For an e-commerce store, it may be harder for a consumer to purchase a high-priced household appliance versus a candy bar. So, it's important to consider these factors when deciding on your attribution window. To change your attribution window, go to the Ads Manager and then click on Settings. Then on the right-hand side of the page, select Edit, drag the slider to your desired click window and view window, and click Save Changes.

You may think that a wider attribution window will give you more accurate results, but unfortunately this just means that Facebook will take more credit for the visits to your website. The reason why is that the algorithm works better with shorter attribution windows. So if you are utilizing non-algorithm based marketing like regularly scheduled tweets or email newsletters, it has been observed that Facebook will take 100% of the referral credit to your website or page. If Facebook is your sole marketing referral outlet on the web, then you have nothing to worry about. But this is something to make note of as you begin analyzing Facebook contributions to the views or sales on your site.

You can also compare Facebook Attribution Windows and create a Campaign Reports if you desire. Once again, this is a great tool if you are running tests to see ads work with your users. To compare these windows, go to Ads Manager and select either the Campaigns, Ad Sets, or Ads folder depending on what data you would like to view. Now, select the Columns menu and click Customize Columns. Here you will be able to select Comparing Windows in the bottom right corner, and then choose the attribution winders under 'view' and 'click' that you want to analyze. Now you can select Apply and see all your results.

Chapter 17: The Psychology of Facebook Ads

There's no denying that Facebook is the leading social media platform in the Western Hemisphere. It's a digital representation of many people's social circles and - for many - their only representation. So it makes sense that advertising on Facebook would be a viable idea. As a mutual place where people look to connect and share their lives, ads on the platform incentives people to "improve
their lives in a place they are already comfortable. But the only difficulty with advertising on Facebook is that its a crowded space with limits in how much you can advertise to people unlike in the real world. Psychologists have found proven strategies to making your ad pop on the site.

On a site built on emotional contingencies and comfortability, it's been proven that emotions always win. So, when cultivating your ad, it may be best to feature a picture or video with a face front and center. No matter what language you speak or what culture you're a part of, a smile is universal. Expressions on a face are often immediate draws to what makes a successful ad on Facebook as it traditionally piques curiosity without much text. While many advertisers will use negative emotions like sadness and despair to trigger the senses of their possible consumers, Facebook has reported that positive displays of emotions are most effect. If people see a smiling face without even seeing the product, they'll be more enticed to click because they connect to the person's story.

Besides emotions, it's been reported that well-known, celebrity faces can also entice consumers to interact with your ad. The sole downfall with this is that Facebook's stringent ad policy may restrict certain celebrities to be featured. You'll just have to get creative in your presentation of this image with your product.

Moreover, when designing the ad itself, color is often an important technique to grabbing audience attention. Most mammals only see 2 colors, but marketing mavens have noted that humans can see 3 and that third color is one of the most important in advertising today. Red - often associated with high energy emotions such as anger or excitement - is a color that grabs such alarming attention that many see the image as a sense. Red's passionate and attention-grabbing nature should be considered for any campaign that vies to stand above from the rest in Facebook's crowded advertising space.

Exclusivities can also assist with making your product more value with consumers. A professor at the University of Maine ran a study that proved the human tendencies to want things that aren't available to everyone. In his study, he had 200 students reveal if they would rather have a cookie from a jar with 10 cookies or a cookie from a jar with 2 cookies. Although both jars featured the exact same cookie, almost all the students preferred the jar with only two cookies. It was perceived that the 2-cookie jar was more valuable, and students didn't want to miss out. So in your ads, using words 'just for you' or 'one-of-a-kind' can certainly improve interactions with ads. We will return to the psychology of words later in this chapter, but presenting scarce and exclusive goods is great way to captivate audiences.

Cognitive dissonance is another tool marketers will use on Facebook to entice users to notice ads. This tactic is when you advertise a conflicting idea from how people perceive themselves or their reality. For instance, if we present evidence that someone is lacking a product that can enhance their quality of life, people feel drawn to wanting to explore why. Behavior analysts have shown that people feel empowered by exploring how they can make their lives better. This self-doubt can often be the catalyst for human beings to want to explore alternative ways of living and ads can deceptively provide a divine moment where people feel like they're being spoken to. Considering people are often alone when using the internet, targeting self-doubt and presenting cognitive dissonance can often be the key to a successful ad on Facebook.

Lastly, text psychology can have an impact on the success rate of an ad. Specific words can create reactions that can be useful in online advertising. While images may still be king when it comes to marketing, specific words can create reactions that can be useful in online advertising.

Free

Free is the ultimate incentive for any viewer of an ad because it immediately alludes that something is being given away. A scientist once ran a test comparing two chocolates; a luxury Lindt truffle for 15 cents and a smaller Hershey's Kiss for 1 cent. Almost everyone who was apart of the study took the Lindt for 15 cents. He then gave those same individuals the option to purchase the same chocolates at a 1 cent discount. This now made the Lindt truffle 14 cents and the Hershey kiss free. Everyone apart of the study chose the Hershey kiss, even though it wasn't their first pick. This is often why free trials are successful with new products as well. People will be more open to trying new things that they don't have to make a financial commitment too.

Save

The word 'save' causes another incentive for people. It has a similar emotional reaction to free because people love being propositioned for discounts through Facebook. Once again, they are already in a considerably safe place on the Internet where they're friends and family are. So, if they are propositioned with the ability to save on an item, they will typically interact with the ad.

Proven

Proven is a effective because it instantly adds value to your product. The word is most effective with software, technologies, or small businesses with little awareness because they are in their infancy. It's also wise not to forget that a lot of Facebook is built on social endorsement. So many will also click on an ad for a Business Page or Website because their friend has simply 'liked' your ad. Seeing the word 'proven' along with a like from one of their friends could be the one-two punch to having a user click on your ad.

New

The newest brands will always have a difficult time establishing themselves because we simply respond to brand we already know in the market. But that doesn't mean that the use of the word 'new' shouldn't be utilized. People love new experiences, food, diets, and places. And if you can target your ad as something innovative or revolutionary to the market rather than inexperienced or unpracticed - you'll have a brand everyone would love to check out.

You

You is one of the most powerful words to use in your ad because it's hyper-personalized. Our minds instantly here our own names when the word 'you' is incorporated into any sentence.

As words continue to be apart of the psychology of Facebook ads, it's worth nothing that people traditionally don't want to be left out. People will also respond to ads that present numbers or social proof in how many users are using your product (or products like yours if you're a new company). You can also use your ad to create a movement that people will want to be apart of. While these are just minor and secondary suggestions for you to capitalize off the psychology of your audience, this is an initial way that you are able to get a jumpstart on capitalizing off attractive ads.

Chapter 18: Creative Best Practices: Copy, Image & Video

As mentioned time and time again, Facebook has an active audience of over 2 billion users. With this, there can be no perfect ad as the audiences are often divided simply by its size. And sure, advertising on Facebook can be an overwhelming feat with every item known to man being featured on the platform. But many ads have thrived in the past by their creative practices alone. So let's unpack some creative tricks and tips that will leave your audience interacting with your ads more than ever.

Today's social media feed is often company to a modern day art gallery. You can see your best friends getting married, your parents on vacation, and - wait - what is this? And ad intruding into my social circles. Many marketers spend months trying to figure out how to eliminate this thought process from happening and encouraging users to think that they need these. Sure, this can be accomplished by actually providing the user something they need. But studies show that with stark imagery that stirs an emotional response from Facebook users, you'll bypass their initial rejection of the ad and accept what it is trying to sell. This is the kind of magnetism that you want your brand to have

Visuals are what immediately peaks our interest when scrolling through an News Feed on our phones. And to reach people quickly on Facebook, the only way for advertisers to successfully do so is visually. Facebook users traditional favor imagery over written text because of the amount of time the audience will have to take to read it. Remember that this is borrowed time you are breaching into when advertising to a new user. Your ad's visuals have to be something they are less likely to forget and more likely to share. This can be done with bright, complementary colors or even present an eye-catching arrangement for the viewer. This is your opportunity to immediately engage with a possible new consumer.

Another tip would be show people using your product. This will immediately pique people's interest because it looks like it belongs in your feed since Facebook is people-based website. Just ensure yourself that your ad doesn't turn off people before actually seeing what you have to offer. Often just featuring your own product will no person will seem like a billboard that no Facebook user will want to interact with. But if you feature a person, studies show that users are more likely to engage in the ad and see what it is all about.

Using words like "This week only" and "Limited-time offer" can help individuals who are unsure if they want to purchase your ad to act on an acting. Setting a deadline to your deal or discount offer, instinctually leads to a conflict in the users mind. People hate missing out on anything and causing this sense of urgency tends to connect with people quicker than just presenting a price. It's also not necessarily every day that people see limited time offers. If every Facebook ad utilized this all the time, the brand would be out of business. So with proper targeting and usage during certain dates, this could elicit quite the response from your audience.

Another general rule of thumb is to leave your Facebook ad pictures free from texts. Facebook used to suggest marketers to include far less than 20% of text overlay on their images. Today, there's no restriction, but as mentioned previously - that may not stop Facebook from not pushing your ads out. It's much more effective to include a short message in the description than intrude on a picture. But if you must include text in your image, Facebook Ads does has a tool that will tell you if your image is approved based off of the amount of text in your image. Also, it's best to make sure these words are offering something to the user like 'SAVE 50% OFF.' This is generally the only time that ads featuring texts will work for the brand engagements. We suggest using a call-to-action button instead to help users shop now on your brand.

Moreover, if you still want to use text in your ad photos, stick to one or two fonts. Too many fonts can make the audience feel overwhelmed and confused by what they are seeing. Remember that you are generally engaging with someone at first glance who does not want to be engaged with at all. You can stick to a standard font for the initial line of text and follow it up with something similar or complementary. But don't go beyond two as this can convolute the overall message of the ad. The idea is to appeal your product or service to this user and not necessarily show off your creativity. Often times, simplicity in the message and design can lead to far greater engagement from your intended audience.

Color design is often a deciding factor for why users will interact with your ad. The following colors are known to elicit certain responses based on the ads:

- Yellow: Often known for optimistic and useful message. Best used with window shoppers.

- Red: Increases heart rate, creates urgency, and represents high energy. Best used for sales or clearances.
- Blue: Creates a sensation of trust and security. Often related to banks or 'brick-and-mortar' businesses.
- Green: Associated with wealth and money, but the easier color for the eyes to process. Stores will often use this to have customers relax.
- Orange: Establishes an aggressive energy and create a call to action to buy, sell, or subscribe to something.
- Pink: Traditionally linked to things romantic or feminine. Often repeated to items that can marketed to women and younger girls.
- Black: Typically establishes power or sleek innovation. Used to market luxury products.
- Purple: Used to sooth or calm. Typically focused on beauty or older audiences looking for anti-aging products.

Lastly, location specific graphics can be important to local business, especially those that are centrally focused on 'word of mouth.' When people see places they know in your ad campaign, they are a much more likely to engage wit your brand. By showcasing the local area to a demographic that is in your local area, you will notice a higher rate in engagement for your business. When GPS and tracking devices were a hot commodity on the market, companies often either targeted local, identifiable images to those in the same communities or worldly, identifiable images to the same individuals. The idea is that the image just had to be identifiable with the user for them to engage.

By using these simple, but effect creative tips, you are on your way to creating a Facebook Ad campaign that will entice hundreds on the platform to engage.

Chapter 19: How to Manage Your Facebook Business Page

We've spoken time and time again about how imperative it is for a business in this age to have a Facebook Business Page. But not just to have one, but to maintain and keep up the page as well. With the platform having over two billion monthly active users, it's almost impossible for a business to go without having a Facebook Business Page that provides the most current information. Do note that this is different a personal profile. Facebook Business Pages allow you to do so much more including advertising, analyzing data, and schedule posts. It's imperative to not only create one, but to utilize all the features that are available.

In order to begin a Facebook page for your business, you first will need to log into your personal Facebook profile and toggle over the Home button next to your name. Here you will be click the Pages tab in the Explore section of the side bar. This will then take you to a main 'Pages' area, where you should click Create Page. Next, you will decide what type of page you would like to create. There are six options including (1) Local Business or Place, (2) Company, Organization or Institution, (3) Brand or Product, (4) Artist, Band or Public Figure, or (5) Entertainment Cause or Community.

Each of these page types will have a drop-down menu with a list of categories you will be able to choose from. It's important to keep in mind that each page has unique category options and will have unique features that only this category will have. So, while it may seem straightforward at first, it's important to look into the different page types and choose which one fits your business best.

After researching the different page type categories, select the Facebook page type and category that will be the best option at this time. If you want to change the category after the page publish, you can always go back to do so. Now, you can fill in the name of your new page along with the other information that Facebook asks for, and select Get Started. Congratulations! You have just created your first Facebook Business Page. Once you click back to your page, you may notice that Facebook has provided some startup tips and ideas in designing a page based on other pages created with your similar category. It's important to read through these tips before inviting others to like your page.

Since it is blank with a lack of information, it is vital to unpublished your page so that you can customize the page before releasing it to the public. In order to do this, select Settings at the top of the navigation bar and open the Page Visibility row in General Settings. You will see Page published and Page unpublished. Toggle over Page Unpublished and click, then elect Save Pages. Now you can focus on building the best Facebook Business Page and reveal it to the public once you are done with the page.

Profile & Cover Photos

Now that you have an unpublished page, you can begin customizing a number of things. Let's start with your profile picture! While we suggest a photo of your physical product or your company logo, you can also use a professional headshot of yourself if you are the face of the business. This may be strategic at first with those you initially invite to your page being unfamiliar with your business. But whatever you decide on, make sure you keep it simple and recognizable. Profile pictures should also be 180 x 180 pixels big to ensure that the picture fits in high quality. You can do this on any image design app or website. Simply change the Custom Dimensions of your design to 180 x 180 and download your image.

If you are ready to upload your image, go back to your Facebook Business page and click Add a Picture in the prompt list. Select the Upload Photo option and follow the designated prompts to upload your new, high quality profile picture. The same can be done with your Facebook cover photo. The one thing to note with this is that dimensions may be different between different platforms (while the profile picture dimensions remain the same). For instance, the dimensions for a Facebook Business Page cover photo on desktop is 828 x 315 pixels.On mobile, the area is 560 x 315 pixel. This means that areas of your cover photo may be hidden on other devices. So it's important to keep in mind that if you want to add words or extensive designs to your cover photo, make sure it's visible on all devices.

When your design is ready, click Add A Cover on the top left corner on the Cover Photo area, and then select Upload Photo. You can also drag the image and position it correctly, and select the Save button once your are happy with your cover photo. Now after you are done uploading, it's important to click on the image and fill in the description. This can be highly valuable real estate for your site, where you can link a landing page, share a tag line, or even quickly introduce new consumers to your business.

Call to Action

A call-to-action button is an accessible way for new consumers to do easy things from signing up for a newsletter to buying products from your line. In order to begin adding your call-to-action button, select Add A Button at the bottom right corner of your cover photo. You will then be prompted to select from several types of standard buttons.

The Get in Touch option has five buttons. The Call Now button allows someone call you with the press of a button. The Contact Us and Sign Up buttons take users to a form on your personal site for lead generation or subscriber capture. The Send Message feature opens a private message exchange between the user and your page.The Send Email button allows users to email you directly from your page.

The Book Services option has two features. The Book Now button allows, which users to book travel or make an appointment, and the Start Order button engages people to order food from your business.

The Learn More option has two features. The Watch Video button directs user to a video on your website or on Facebook. The Learn More button will often show users more info on your business.

The Make a Purchase or Donation has a single feature. The Shop Now button allows more people to see and buy products.

The Download App or Game option has two features. The Use App button brings people to your app and will increase downloads or engagement. The Play Game button lets people download or play your game. From these options, you will be able to see what fits best for your business.

Description

While many businesses typically look over creating a description for this page, it's actually one of the most important features of your page because it gives information to potential followers. Although you're only limited to 155 characters, it's imperative to use this limited amount of words since this section will show up in search results and help your SEO ranking for consumers looking for new product. To add your own Short Description, click on Add a Short Description and write two sentence when prompted to under the Welcome to Your Page splash page. Then click Save and you've just moved your page up the ranks in the search engine optimization wars.

Custom Usernames

Every Facebook page will be given a unique URL once it is created, but it's important to continue marketing your brand and this is the easiest way to do so. You can customize the latter portion of your Facebook URL with a unique username that should be your business name. Unless your brand name is an acronym or abbreviations, remember to stay away from them since you want brand identity.

Other Settings

After you've finished creating your business page, it's time to focus on secure your site from the backend form giving certain people access to managing the page, and so on.

Under the general settings listing, we suggest enabling shortcuts to pin at the top of your Facebook page for easy accessibility to your business page. You can also choose who to allow to publish posts, pictures, and videos on your page under Visitor Posts. You can also check Review Posts by Other People to review each post before they are published. Inviting others to post Visitor Posts may encourage interaction and a personal connection with your company at first. You can also give people the ability to ask questions through Messenger. While we will discuss Messenger Bots later, you canticle the Messages box that shows the Message button on your page. This will motivate users to interact more with your brand even further.

To increase your visibility, you can also toggle over the Others Tagging this Page box - which will allow people and other business pages to share and tag your page. Not only will this expand audiences, but it will allow consumers to feel more connected. In connection to this, you can also restrict certain ages from seeing or interacting with your page if you are selling age-sensitive products. Furthermore, you can block comments that feature certain words. From names of competition to profanity, you are able to control the image of your business - even if it is through the words of your followers. Lastly, if you do want your page to appear whenever they search certain topics or pages - you can toggle over the Similar Page Suggestions box to have Facebook suggest your page to users as their relevant searches.

You can also update your audience whenever you change details like phone numbers, websites, or descriptions. This can be done by editing the Page Updates settings to reflect what's best for your brand.

Messaging settings could also be quite attractive in promoting your business. If someone was to send you a private message through your page, you have an option to activate the Response Assistant to deliver automated responses. These messages are customized to your user name and you can even edit the template copy to align with your brand's voice. While not as intricate as chatbots, you will be able to confirm that you've receive a message, let consumers know that you're out of the office, or simply thanking Messenger users for contacting your page. If you are looking for more in-depth auto-response systems, you should certainly look into Messenger Bots

Chapter 20: What are Messenger Bots?

Chat bots have been around for the past decade and are replacing everything from email marketing to customer service agents. They also allow individual to cut costs on labor and increase their revenue. Simply put, they do what many companies need without hiring the labor and training to do so. According to Oracle, 80 percent of all businesses will have an automated chatbot in place by 2020. It's not a shock since these automated systems are programmed to receive questions, provide answers, and then execute tasks efficiently. Rather than wait for an establishment to open or deal with a human who may not have all the answers, customers are typically open to working with these chatbots since they are so informed. While they may not be able to convey the same emotional connection a human can, they get the job done and in an efficient way. Facebook Messenger Bots are very similar. The only bonus is that virtually everyone in the world has Facebook, so these bots can be beneficial because consumers can interact with your business from the comforts of a platform they are already familiar with. Facebook Messenger is the third-most used app in world with 68 percent of app users using the device. While wise to, there's often no reason for online businesses to offer an alternative means for customer service or FAQs. This can save costs and time for any new business.

Facebook Messenger Bots are also a far less competitive field than Facebook Ads. Although over 6 million advertisers using Facebook Ads, only 300,000 are currently using chatbots. And with marketing emails on the details on the decline, chat bots are the new digital frontier for direct communication on the Internet. Studies have shown that consumers are 3.5 times more likely to open a Facebook Message than a marketing email. Marketing email click-through rates are currently at an astonishing 3.1% with only a third of all marketing emails being opened. Times are changing and it appears that chatbots are the future of hyper-intensive marketing. Also, Facebook Messenger even has sponsored ads now that can be sen to anyone who has been in touch with your page. This means that you already have a subscriber list without telling users to sign up.

As mentioned perviously, Facebook Messenger Bots can also save you time and money on customer care. In today's internet age, consumers are expecting round the clock availability and often hate waiting on hold. They also ask the same questions again and again since they don't have a central place where they can ask these questions without picking up the phone or even emailing a live agent. These chatbots not only allows your company to free up time and focus, but can instantly solve the problems of your consumers.

Now while it may seem like these bots are simple answer portals, they can actually serve many things for your business. Aside from the traditional customer care, Messenger Bots have the ability to book appointments, track packages, and even suggest the best outfit for you to wear once it receives the proper measurements. Marriott currently uses chatbots to allow guests to book their future reservations and even has a specified careers chatbot for the millennial job seeker who may be looking for a new career path. Moreover, cosmetic retailer Sephora uses chatbots to book in-store makeovers. The service has been so well-received that booking rates have increased by 11 percent and tend to tip their artists more since they've implemented the chatbots. Sephora also does giveaways through Messenger Bots including free makeovers by random selection. It's an incentive that keeps their customers wanting to communicate with the brand digitally rather than calling into a store or hotline. Once again, this allows the company to focus their labor and training on other things than just answering remedial questions on the phone.

Now with all this data showing success stories with implementing chatbots, you may be wondering how you can create one of your very own. Well fortunately, chat bots are quite easily to create from self-serving tool to ones for companies with bigger budgets for developers, etc. We give you a guide to the different free and user-friendly Messenger Bot sites currently out there so that you can find one perfect for your company.

Streamchat

Streamchat is a popular and one of the easier chatbot tools available. It's meant for those looking for simple auto responses like "Out of the office" or "Will be back soon" rather than to manage broader workflows or incorporate booking capabilities. Streamchat is also a good tool to try on your consumers before enlisting a larger server.

Chatfuel

Chatfuel is a large self-serve platform that was made for Facebook Messenger bots specifically.

While many of the other self-service chatbot platforms can be used virtually on any platform, Chatfuel has Facebook users and coding in mind. It also has quite the client list with NFL teams, Netflix, and TechCrunch having enlisted the service to provide their Facebook Messenger a chat bot service. Chatfuel is also free for those who do not have coding backgrounds. Of course you can sign up for Chatfuel Pro if you would like to edit the front end of the boy and add customizable options, but this is up to you. The Pro version does cost, but it's more those businesses who already have a rapport with their consumers in this way on the platform. Chatfuel also features a broadcasting feature that allows you to send messages to multiple users at once. So if you were to incorporate a giveaway or announcements into your chatbot, Chatfuel is a great tool to utilize.

MobileMonkey

MobileMonkey is a free service that allows you to build your own Facebook Messenger bot with a myriad of features from Live Chat Takeover to Pre-Automated Q&A triggers and templates They also have a similar feature to Chatfuel's called ChatBlast, where you can talk to multiple users at once. You can also schedule these ChatBlast's out ahead of time, which is apart of their Pro plan. You will also be able to see key analytics if you were to upgrade as well.

Moreover, if you are not satisfied with these free Messenger Bot services - you can certainly hire a developer and look into other Enterprise tools. Chatkit, Reply.Al, The Bot Platform, Conversable, and even Facebook Messenger for Developers can be complementary tools to help your developers build the perfect chatbot for your business. The Bot Platform is a builder that new or self-taught developers will use since it doesn't require coding. It's also currently used by many notable brands around the world from BBC to Sony due to its reliability and simplicity in building chats. Once again, these won't be quite as easy as the easy builders listed previously. But they are great starting points for you to begin connecting to your audience through adverts and automated systems.

Chapter 21: Facebook Resources You Can Use to Up Your Game

WhatsApp

Acquired in 2014, WhatsApp is Facebook latest resource to help you your game on the platform. Similar to Facebook Messenger, WhatsApp is a personalized form of messages, but generally associated with many people's friends and colleagues. With over 1.6 billion users, WhatsApp provides businesses a unique opportunity to connect with their customers and have genuine conversations. Small businesses currently use the app as an unconventional for owners to communicate with their customers in a hand-to-hand combat approach to marketing. Unfortunately, WhatsApp doesn't have the same advertisement model that Facebook does today. But with it being WhatsApp's parent company, it appears that it's only a matter of time. Which is why it would be wise for any business to connect to WhatsApp's audiences today, so that they have a build-in network once Facebook launches on the site.

WhatsApp is also a highly personal communication that many users feel brands shouldn't be apart of. While this can generally make it less accessible for businesses to connect with their audiences, if they approach customers as their friends - it may work. There simply has to be a delicate balance with the consumer. If users feel like brands are intruding on their personal spaces, they may alienate a company all together. But if done properly, this could be an untapped resource on Facebook to not only build a new Customer List. But build a relationship with an established client.

The Audience Network

Previously we've discussed the power in the placements of your ad on Facebook. The Audience Network serves ads both on and off the Facebook platform such as on mobile apps like WhatsApp. But this network is the only placement option where marketers generally can't decide where their ads are placed. When you decide what format and where to place your Facebook ads, you know exactly where your ad is being shown. On Facebook, ads are shown in a variety of ways. But if served incorrectly without the proper scaling of your ad, you could essentially may damage your brand. But this is what the Audience Network is for.The reason every brand needs to put at least some effort in your campaign is because if it works, you can scale your campaigns in a competition-free placement three to five times faster than any other placement on Facebook. The Audience Network can be the ad saving resource you never knew you needed.

Instagram

While Facebook has refocused their content to family and friends, their photo-based partner and simplistic app called Instagram has allowed it to naturally because the new home of brands. Plus, it's actually easier for company's to promote on the platform with higher engagement, followers focused more on following brands than people, and businesses actually achieving their goals in connection. Now while Instagram is an incredible tool, we're not at all suggesting that you should abandon or spend less time on your Facebook Ads audience. But it may be wise to start refining your strategies to including other social media platforms and engaging with more users as a result.

If you don't already have an Instagram account, it's important to get one. But most do - so you can simply convert it to an Instagram business account in a matter of clicks. This will give you the opportunity to track existing followers and see analytics on how your account should be performing to encounter more engagement. You could also create a separate Instagram business account. To do so, download the Instagram app for any phone device. Open the app and click Sign Up. Here it will ask for your email address. Once you do this, select Next and be sure to connect your Instagram business account to your Facebook Business Page by logging into Facebook. This is important in not only creating brand unity on social media, but because Facebook owns Instagram. It will give you the accessibility to operate between the two platforms.

Now you will choose your username and password and select Done. If you are looking to convert your existing personal Instagram to a Business account, log in and select the three-lined icon at the upper right corner of your screen and choose Settings. Here you'll select Switch to Business Profile, and tap Continue. For any business account, you must include an email address, phone number, or physical address to complete your profile. And now you're done.

The simplicity of Instagram being a photo app is that it's easier to decide what kind of content you want people to see since it can only be an image or video. Sure, you can include text in your posts with no restrictions unlike Facebook. But this isn't recommended since Instagram is mostly known for their pictures. The majority of Instagram audience is also under 35 with an even split between male and female users. So this may be useful information when understanding how exactly you would like to promote your brand on the platform. And since understanding your target audience is one of the most imperative thing with any marketing strategy, it's definitely important to do the same for Instagram.

Once you've created your account and defined your audience on the platform, your audience will now expect to see you post regularly on the platform. You will want to keep them engaged with your brand without overwhelming them to the point that they quit paying attention - or even worst, unfollow you. While once studied, there's not one time that is best to post for all businesses. It's best to do a trial run of posting engaging content and seeing what are the best hours for your brands. It may also not be wise to compare your engagement to those of other brands. Of course, a brand with a higher follower count is going to have more likes out the gate than your new feed. But even beyond that, if you see that the metrics are better for a similar business in the morning and you don't see the same results - it may be because this brand has trained their audience to expect uploads during this time. The key observation is to see when your users are online. Understand that your followers may also not be online at the same time you are. Fortunately, Instagram allows you to see exactly when your followers are online by the day. So it may be wise to only post photos accordingly based on these high engagement times.

To get to this information, open your Instagram Business Profile and select the three bars icon on the upper right and select Insights. Then tap on the Audience Tab and you will be able to see these active times. It's often recommended to take this information and create a digital calendar to plan when you are going to post. Another thing is to make sure you properly update your Instagram bio. By creating a brand voice and using hashtags, you will be able to connect with an Instagram audience deeply and convey exactly what your brand is. If your brand allows, you may also want to use emojis or line breaks. Remember that Instagram is majorly used by the Millennial crowd who prefers certain grammar techniques than different platforms.

Your profile picture is also important in connecting your audience to your brand. Choose a profile picture that you feel is going to be identifiable with your business. You can use the same profile picture across all accounts, but just make sure it's high resolution on all platforms. For example, a proper Instagram profile pic displays as 110 x 110 pixels, but is stored at 320 x 320. It's a good idea to make sure your profile picture is some version of your logo.

Besides the utilization of a profile picture, it's wise to use all the components of your business account. This includes names, usernames, and website links as well. You would be surprised to find how many Instagram users mistakenly only use their username in their profiles. It's important to have your name as well since this helps search engine optimization externally, but also helps users who may be unfamiliar with your username to find your brand. It's also imperative to have your username be the same or similar as the name of your company. Do the same with your website link and you're on your way to crafting a professional Instagram business account.

Now, the most important thing with any Instagram account is to share great content. Before posting anything to your page, think about how this contributes to your brand. If you offer a service, try showing some consumer stories through a unique hashtag. Or through your Instagram stories, go behind the curtain of your office and invite your followers that way. People love to feel like they're apart of the journey and the earlier they become a part of it, the longer they're likely to be committed.

After deciding on theming and proper content, it's important to create a consistent visual look. Consistent colors and an overall aesthetic will make uses feel at home on your Instagram feed. This also helps your brand stand out from the other ones. And you don't even need to commit to expensive photography equipment. Some of the best Instagram photos can be taken from your smartphone. And through mobile photo editing apps like VSCOcam, you can prove your feed additional filters and love that your competition may not be using. Just make sure your brand is recognizable, distinct, and contributing back to your overall goal - which is a conversion or sale for your company. By using using natural light taking balanced photos, you've starting building your online presence even more.

Building an audience on Instagram can be quite simple once you've determined what your theme and message is going to be on the platform. The secret is by using the personal touches on the platform and being committed to following through on your posts. For instance, instead of solely posting videos on your feed, try communicating through Instagram stories. Instagram is a great app where you can commit to your audience to the story of your brand. Just be consistent when using the feature and remember the more you engage directly with customers, the more likely they'll engage back. You can also extend your Instagram stories beyond 24 hours through Instagram Stories Highlights. This will allow users new and old to return to your page to review information that you may posted about the brand.

Even though Instagram is about the imagery and visuals, it's important to not forget about the captions underneath the images. Captions allow you to tell a story that will inherently make you photo meaningful. Captions can also make followers feel connected to the brand emotionally. It also allows you to create an identifiable brand voice. Once again, you are promoting yourself generally to the under 35 crowd - so are there emojis that you want to use to engage with them? Is there a campaign you would like to start through a series of customizable hashtags? Maybe there's some choices in grammar you would like to utilize to connect with this audience a little bit intimately. With Instagram being majorly used on mobile devices, it would be wise to talk to your audience like they are your personal friends or confidants. Professionally, of course. But if you commit to a style, you can definitely cultivate a tone and connection your desired audience.

Social networking is just that - an online network and community, so they should be treated as such. A group of people relevant to your brand is already on Instagram. You just have to look for them and engage into them like community leaders do. One way is to follow people or brands they follow and study how they connect with their audience. You can also closely look into industry hashtags and comment on relevant posts. This is often attractive to audiences looking for new brands to follow when they see other brands commenting on the brands they are currently following. As you get more connected to the different communities on Instagram, you will begin to understand which tactics elicit the best responses.

Using the right hashtags will also allow audiences to discover your posts on Instagram. While captions aren't searchable, hashtags are. When someone taps on a hashtag, they are able to see pages of associated content. So typically, you will be able to get your content in front of Instagram users who typically don't follow your brand. You may also want to consider creating your own unique hashtag that embodies the essence of your brand and has your followers support you. This can also create a unique feed of generated content that will build a community beyond those who follow you. Instagram also allows you to follow hashtags now too, which allows companies to evolve beyond just their pages. They can create a movement if they're innovative in their presentation.

Moreover, while it does seem tedious, you must reply to all comments and mentions (if you can in the beginning). Often with social media, brands get so consumed with creating aesthetically pleasing feeds and the visual that they lose the connection. It's called social media for a reason and most lose the most vital part, which is being social. And while bots can be great for Facebook Messenger, using bots to reply to Instagram comments never works out well on the platform. It will just create a distance with your audience. Because while users on Facebook are looking for questions to simply be answers, audiences on Instagram prefer the direct engagement.

You can also try working with "influencers" on the platform to help promote your business. These influencers already have an engaged fanbase who they can make interested in your brand. Of course, you'd want to focus on connecting with these personalities who's brands generally overlap. You will find more of an engaged audience if you do it this way. And you won't even need a large budget to do this. You can stick to a smaller influence with a limited but dedicated following.

Lastly, try connecting your Instagram page into other platforms like Facebook or your online blog. You obviously want people to know about your Instagram business account. If you give your audience a preview of the content that you're going to offer, they'll be more likely to follow. Also, embedding your Instagram account into your blog is quite easy on my templated platforms. If not, try including your Instagram handle in your business emails or on analog materials like business cards and flyers. This will not only lead to the organic engagement from your current supporters, but it will elicit them to search for you on other platforms as well. With social media, you always want followers to feel like they can consume your brand or product identity at any time of day. Engagement is your goal and building an online audience with more brand accessibility can get you it.

With these tips as well as the ones listed in previous chapters, you have been taught how to utilize Facebook Ads to skyrocket your business to new heights.